Bob taught these principles on identity in Christ to my staff and I years ago. The truths that he shared with us have influenced me as much if not more than any other teaching I've encountered in my life. It has radically deepened and strengthened my marriage, parenting, teaching, discipleship, counseling, and evangelism. I believe this is true for many of my staff team and the college students we seek to minister to as well.

-Olan Stubbs, *Campus Outreach* Birmingham Regional Director

In this book Bob Smart calms us afresh with the assurances of who we most deeply are in Jesus Christ. Bob takes us into the very core of what it means to be in Jesus Christ, nestling us into the remarkable claim of the gospel that we have been freely adopted by the Father and have nothing to prove and nothing to lose.

-Dane Ortlund, Executive Vice President of Bible Publishing for Crossway Publications

The Gospel of Christ renovates people's lives as they grow in an intimate knowledge of Jesus and the identity He gives them. After personally going through Dr. Smart's teaching on Identity in Christ and finding it very helpful, we decided to incorporate it as part of our church-wide discipleship. Christians deeply struggle from believing various condemning message which become the identity by which they live. Messages such as, "I am unloveable", or "I'm not good enough", set them on a course of performance to gain what the Gospel has already given them; acceptance, love, belonging and ultimately an identity. The Identity study has enabled people in our church to not only believe, but to also live according to who God says they are and not giving anyone else a vote.

-Rusty Milton, Senior Minister of Grace Presbyterian Church of Christchurch, New Zealand

Peter was asked of Jesus, "Who do you say I am?" Peter's answer honored the authority, relationship, and Truth of who his Savior was to him, and to the world. Dr. Smart has written an excellent book calling us forth to answer the same question Jesus asks all of his followers, and then in turn, just as he did for

Peter, tells us who we are. You shall be called Peter . . . Bob unpacks the very blocks (CCTs) or core lies and strategies we believe, and he shows us a way to encounter the Living God and to experience freedom. Thank you, friend, for such a timely and wise book.

-Kimberly D. Knochel, MABC Counselor and Consultant newdayinitiative.com

Embracing Your Identity in Christ:

RENOUNCING LIES AND FOOLISH STRATEGIES

ROBERT DAVIS SMART

WESTBOW
PRESS®
A DIVISION OF THOMAS NELSON
& ZONDERVAN

WestBow Press books may be ordered through booksellers or by contacting:

WestBow Press
A Division of Thomas Nelson & Zondervan
1663 Liberty Drive
Bloomington, IN 47403
www.westbowpress.com
1 (866) 928-1240

ISBN: 978-1-5127-7889-2 (sc)
ISBN: 978-1-5127-7890-8 (hc)
ISBN: 978-1-5127-7888-5 (e)

Library of Congress Control Number: 2017903846

Print information available on the last page.

WestBow Press rev. date: 04/28/2017

Contents

Acknowledgments vii

Foreword ix

Introduction: The First of Four Seasons of Gospel
           Transformation xiii

Chapter 1   The Genesis of Your Identity 1

Chapter 2   Gender Redeemed 17

Chapter 3   The Interpretation War 28

Chapter 4   Acceptance 43

Chapter 5   No Longer Fatherless 51

Chapter 6   Set Apart as Special to God 57

Chapter 7   Adorable in God's Sight 62

Conclusion: Giving Testimony 67

Bibliography 71

Appendix 1: Cherishing Lies about Our Identities as Ministry
           Leaders 77

Appendix 2: Self-Hatred 83

Appendix 3: Justification 85

Acknowledgments

My deep thanks to Christ Church staff and members, *Cru*, *InterVarsity*, and *Navigator* campus staff, and those involved in the last twenty years of spiritual formation classes locally for sharing your precious sense of identity in Christ from the heart. I am also grateful to *Campus Outreach* staff and leaders in Alabama, Louisiana, Illinois, and Texas for using this material for years at various summer projects. I am indebted to Rev. Rusty Milton of Grace Presbyterian and *Grace Theological College* in New Zealand for using this material in local ministry settings, and offering good feedback.

I am particularly glad to have discussed in depth aspects of the demonic with the late Rev. Brad Bush of the Lafayette, IN Christian Missionary Alliance. Finally, this and many projects could not be possible without the constant encouragement from Gary and Farole Haluska.

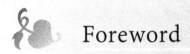 # Foreword

Once, a night-storm caught several followers of Jesus unawares on a boat. To make matters worse, they saw in their struggle, a specter seeking their doom upon the waters. "It is a ghost!" they cried, vulnerable to the spook and the waves.

But just then, familiar voice, pierced through what troubled them. "It is I don't be afraid," said the voice. To their surprise, what they thought was a ghost to haunt them, turned out to be Jesus earnest to save them.

Sometimes things frighten us and rightly so. A ghost is a ghost. But sometimes what frightens us isn't what we think it is. Sometimes what looks bad to us is actually good, coming to save us.

When I first met Bob Smart, I wanted little to do with him. I was a college student. He was a Campus Minister. I wore accomplishments and carried potential. He wore a big smile and carried a large black Bible. I tried to cover my broken soul with religion. He sought to uncover his broken soul and point both of us to Jesus.

Though I wanted authenticity I had not encountered his kind before. I was cynical and frightened by it. Bob was like a ghost to me. But through Bob's life, I came to see that it was actually Jesus arriving for the both of us, all along. Bob knew that. He wanted me to know it too.

In those early days, I heard Bob and his wife Karen laugh and play. I saw them cry and pray. I saw them argue with one another and forgive each other. Their living room was open to me. Within its simple colonial style decoration, I learned to make Spaghetti, hold a baby, play games as a family and seek Jesus from the heart in ordinary places among ordinary people.

In the days since, I've met the son-in-laws and daughters-in-law he prayed for in an empty church near Wayne Street, when his kids were just toddlers or not yet born. And I've heard the content of this book spoken to me along my various and tumultuous threats to my identity in Jesus from Indiana to Ohio to Missouri.

No man is a perfect one. Like you and me, Bob is no exception. He too is a "glorious ruin" who with us, looks to Jesus. But I don't know where I'd be without Bob Smart seeking to find the kind of language you are about to read, and using it to speak tenderly of Jesus throughout my life. I don't know where I'd be without Bob seeking imperfectly but earnestly to live such things himself and welcoming me tangibly into his and Karen's lives. They helped me hear and see what the lover of our souls sounds like and talks like.

Mine has been a life dismantled by divorces. As a child of my parents and as an Adult myself. Identity gets lost amid these and the many other kinds of traumas inflicted upon us and too, if we live long enough, the many that we inflict upon others. Imposter identities offer themselves to us amid such wanderings. We often choose their thievery. We lose our way. We lose sight of God and of ourselves as God created and knows us to be. It is the grace of God that he sends us companions for these paths; spiritual friends who help us grow attentive to Jesus and receive His recovering of us.

Jesus has given Bob grace and gifting to help us hear the voice of the One who comes upon the waters. The one who sounds at first like a ghost in the night storms, but who is in truth, the Lord Himself, declaring peace, amid his strong rescue. From there in the night storms, He brings us safely home. And we who love Him tell the story of our identity. We are those for whom the steadfast love of the Lord, never quits.

Zack Eswine
Pastor of Riverside Church, Webster Groves, Missouri
Director of Homiletics, Covenant Theological Seminary
January 23, 2017

Introduction

The First of Four Seasons of
Gospel Transformation

Identity in Christ

Our identities, besides being one of the most precious things to protect from theft, crisis, or loss, are extremely important to God. The Father has given each of His children a personal identity in Christ that will shape them on their journey to heaven. If, in the process of identity formation, we ignore what God says concerning our identities, then we may expect confusion in the other three seasons of spiritual formation, from adolescence to old age (see chart below for Calling *to* Christ, Intentionality *for* Christ, and Legacy *from* Christ).

4 SEASONS OF SPIRITUAL FORMATION

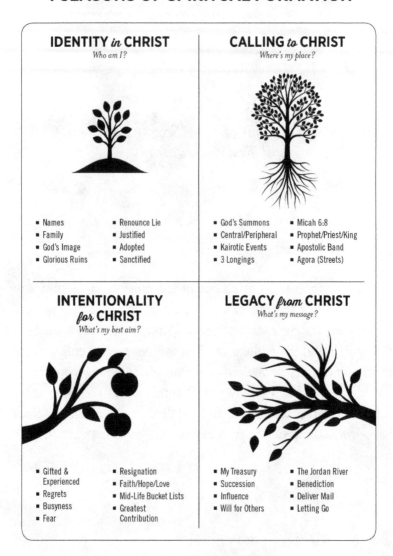

IDENTITY *in* CHRIST
Who am I?

- Names
- Family
- God's Image
- Glorious Ruins
- Renounce Lie
- Justified
- Adopted
- Sanctified

CALLING *to* CHRIST
Where's my place?

- God's Summons
- Central/Peripheral
- Kairotic Events
- 3 Longings
- Micah 6:8
- Prophet/Priest/King
- Apostolic Band
- Agora (Streets)

INTENTIONALITY *for* CHRIST
What's my best aim?

- Gifted & Experienced
- Regrets
- Busyness
- Fear
- Resignation
- Faith/Hope/Love
- Mid-Life Bucket Lists
- Greatest Contribution

LEGACY *from* CHRIST
What's my message?

- My Treasury
- Succession
- Influence
- Will for Others
- The Jordan River
- Benediction
- Deliver Mail
- Letting Go

Just after birth or adoption, a child is given her first sense of identity from her parent(s). Identity formation, however, is a much longer process. When Jesus Christ was approximately thirty years of age, the Father spoke of His identity at His baptism just before He entered fully into His primary calling. In the same way, a clear sense of our identity in Christ ought to precede our calling formation to Christ. It is during this foundational season of identity formation that Satan challenges each of us, as he did our Lord. The devil's first attacks were aimed at Jesus's identity when two times he cast doubt about His identity: *"If* you are the Son of God ..."* (Luke 4:3, 9).[1]

The evil trinity—the world, the flesh, and the devil—is seeking to kill and destroy us during each of the four seasons of spiritual formation. In the spring evil confuses our identities, in the summer our callings, in the autumn our intentionality, and in the winter our legacies. The world escorts us to the pit, the flesh entices us to fall in, and the devil pushes us over the edge. "The pit," as it were, represents a dark and slimy collection of lies, condemning thoughts, and foolish strategies designed to confuse, distort, and manage our identity formation, to no avail.

This first season of spiritual formation for the Christian, identity in Christ, is the first of four seasons of gospel transformation designed to shape us into the glorious likeness of Jesus Christ. The Bible favors beginning here before asking the next three major questions of the Christian life: Where's my place (calling)? How do I steward all my gifts, resources, and efforts well in the light of eternity (intentionality)? What inheritance, testament, and benediction do I leave behind as I prepare to cross the river of death to gain eternity (legacy)?

Embracing your true identity in Christ has much more weight than you may give it at this time. It is foundational as a teenager, formational during our twenties and thirties, and progressively solidifying for all Christians until we come to cross the river of death.

My Story

It has been a delight to teach this material over the years in churches and seminaries and among campus ministry leaders. Older adults may experience new freedom and, with tears, wish they had discovered this when they were younger. God is sovereign on the timing of discovery too. Realizing its importance grew out of my story, my own struggle with Satan's lie or a central condemning thought. What seemed so painfully true of me, yet so irrational to my closest family and friends, was indeed a lie. Evil's condemnation felt so true about who I was, even in the face of truth. This core lie, or *central condemning interpretation* (CCT),[2] seemed ever present the more I followed my call and attempted to overcome it. At times I was driven to prove it was not true of me with more effort and spiritual disciplines, but I was still ruled by the lie. When it seemed like it was no use trying any longer, I occasionally surrendered to it. Either way, evil's interpretation of me, enforced by the law, ruled my Christian performance more than the gospel. In time I was able to spell out the lie and see how it repeatedly made sense at significantly painful events in my life. I couldn't understand my own commitment to the lie and the depth of deceit by simply rehearsing the truth. The serious struggle with the timing, nature, and function of deceit led to the following conviction; namely, we each actually cherish a central condemning thought about ourselves more than we are willing to admit. We actually cherish our core lie! Why? This is because it has often functioned for a long time to give us a sense of success, but never enough. We eventually find ourselves surrendering to an identity of condemnation in the end. Our foolish strategies support the false illusion that our default mode of operation (personal autonomy) can overcome Satan's message of condemnation. After

---

[2] Dave Bowman of the Navigators has helped me tremendously on this point. He trained me at Purdue in the 1980s.

I discovered how my false identity functioned for me, I was able to name the foolish strategies that were used to overcome it. It sounds too good to be true, but by taking our condemning thoughts about ourselves and foolish strategies captive, and by believing the gospel each day, we are able to enjoy the stable, full, and solid Christian life Jesus promised us (John 10:10). In fact, we cannot love well when our "ministry to others" is all about overcoming our own sense of condemnation.

How to Use This Book in Small Groups

This book will help you with your identity, story, and calling as a Christian—each spiritual formation season from now until the end. It addresses our common struggles with self-hatred, depression, powerlessness, people pleasing, and self-righteousness. It offers solid help for those with gender confusion, same-sex attractions, and racial issues. When you read about the simplicity of daily repenting of lies and renouncing foolish strategies that did and do not work and often preaching the gospel to yourself, a strong conviction will grow in the core of your being about who you really are in Christ. The truth is that the gospel is sufficient. Although there is nothing more than the gospel, there is certainly more of it to nourish us beyond baby's milk as the meat to strengthen the mature. The gospel is the milk for the young and the meat for the mature Christian. The way this book nuances Christian experience will help you embrace the gospel in new ways and actually increase your performance in Christian obedience, good works, and calling to Christ. For you *are* God's workmanship, created to fulfill good works predestined for you to do (Ephesians 2:10). A stronger sense of your Christian identity will set you up for living intentionally *for* Christ in midlife and pass on to others a legacy *from* Christ in old age. A basic leader's guide and group discussion questions are provided at the end of each chapter.

Why This Book?

All people are reluctant to face their pathologies; Christians, surprisingly, seem to despise the depth and reality of evil. Although there have been plenty of books written on identity in Christ (some better than others),[3] it became clear that another portion of Christian arsenal could benefit us. Beyond listing the essential and wonderful identity declarations, (like "I am justified," etc.), readers will benefit from knowing how their genders, ethnicities, genealogies, and stories relate to who they are. Christians must not simply mount truth on top of their underlying deceit; they must first become unpleasantly aware of what other messages have been ruling them. They must not only realize the nature, timing, and function of deceit; they must renounce Satan's lies with the gospel's God-given authority in God's presence. When the Psalmist repented and found forgiveness and freedom from condemnation, he embraced God's deep desire—namely, God desires truth in one's inmost being (Ps. 51:6).

Chapter 1 begins with some givens about you, which is intended to make you take ownership of what God says about you, your name, your ethnicity, and your uniqueness. It begins with your glory as an image-bearer.

Chapter 2 unpacks what it means that people are made in God's image by differentiating us according to our genders. It looks at the glory, the ruin, and the redemption of masculinity and femininity. Chapter 3 explains the interpretation war in every believer's mind and heart between truth and deceit—what Satan and God tell you

---

[3] See book reviews at http://www.identityinchrist.co/reviews.

about who you are. It explains the twofold way of identity-repentance that must precede our exercise of identity—faith in the gospel way of identity formation in Christ.

Chapters 4 through 7 highlight the gospel's authoritative interpretation about who we are as Christians. Finally, readers will enjoy using the conclusion's template to spell out their individual and personal identities in Christ. This is my aim: that you each truly embrace your identity in Christ, spell out your false and true identities, and share this with others in your group. For this to happen in the best possible way, I recommend that you utilize the supplemental discussion questions designed for you to enjoy in small groups or life-on-life missional discipleship (LOLMD). It is in this context that we have known the Holy Spirit to fall upon us—when people share their identities in Christ with others within the context of Christian community and in local churches where the gospel is delighted in most.

For ongoing interaction and more resources, please see my blog at http://www.identityinChrist.co.

Questions for Group Discussions for Leaders

1. Introduce yourselves by going around and sharing your full names. Ask the following questions.
2. What are you looking forward to in this study?
3. Why is this an important season to embrace your true identity in Christ at this time?
4. What are some of your fears?

Chapter 1
The Genesis of Your Identity

The Central Question of Authority

The central question of first importance for beginning a vital, lifelong, gospel-transformational process is the question of authority. The cacophony of voices must be silenced and named, for we are ruled by the interpretation that we have given the greatest authority to rule our lives. *Who have you given the authority to tell you just who you are?* Is it a person you respect? Is it a bully's message from your past that is still ruling you? Who is the only one who has this authority? Does your loved one or your supervisor's message govern you? Do you think you have the authority to give yourself your own identity? All these sources of authority, however close they are to the truth, will not lead you into freedom and transformation fitting for your glory in Christ. For only God (the gospel) has the authority to answer the most important question of life—namely, "Who am I?"

Although Western culture has supported radical individualism (that we each decide for ourselves who we are without an outside source of authority), the gospel does not.[4] If one attempts to answer the personal identity question autonomously, then that person has no outside authority to help bring solid security about his or her identity. One of the most helpful thinkers to help us understand our time is Dr. Charles Taylor. Taylor has identified five conditions of contemporary culture, which makes a person experience isolation, agnosticism, confusion, oppression, and insignificance with regard to identity. Christians are finding it increasingly complex to embrace their true identities in Christ in contemporary culture, which Taylor describes in five conditions.

Five Conditions of Our Age[5]

First, Taylor argues that the "Buffered Self," not the "Porous Self" of the premodern age, is the norm. By buffered, he means that contemporary people do not view themselves as vulnerable to messages, spells, interventions, or powers from the unseen world outside themselves. Taylor believes that modern people's default mode is to doubt the Christian faith.

Second, Taylor asserts that contemporary people have the possibility for the first time to imagine "exclusive humanism," which claims to account for meaning and significance without any reference or appeal to God or transcendence. Exclusive humanism asserts that people are basically good and that humanity can solve the world's problems without turning to any unseen god for help. We must answer the question of identity within ourselves. Humanism has been described by one preacher as a cheerleading squad, whose team is trailing behind without any hope of winning, chanting: "We can do it! We can do it! We can. We can!"

---

[4] See Ken Myers's resources: http://reformedforum.org/20-years-of-the-mars-hill-audio-journal/.

[5] Charles Taylor, *A Secular Age* (Cambridge, MA: Belknap Press, 2007), 28–34.

Third, Taylor believes that believers of all religions are fragile. Why? "The fragilization of believers" is indicative of all believers because there are too many expressions of belief, and a handful of contesting narratives are constantly knocking on the door of one's belief system at any given moment. We live in an age of doubt, which makes fundamentalist atheists and assured believers suspect to all.

Fourth, we modern (postmodern) people are "encased in *Chronos*" (this moment), and live only "the tick-tock" of time without any sense of *Kairos* (time from God's perspective). This makes it hard for a Christian to believe that painful events or redemptive moments are pregnant with significance with regard to naming one's identity.[6]

Finally, Taylor assumes that we deny God's active involvement in our daily lives. He calls this "the Immanent Frame" where immanentization has eclipsed God's providence (God sustaining and governing all that He created). Just as Francis Schaeffer stated that modern man in the twentieth century began to live without an infinite, transcendent reference point (God),[7] so Taylor sees immanentization as the process whereby meaning, significance, and "fullness" (the good life) are sought within an enclosed, self-sufficient,

---

[6] Taylor writes: "We define our identity always in dialogue with, sometimes in struggle against, the things our significant others want to see in us. Even after we outgrow some of these others—our parents, for instance—and they disappear from our lives, the conversation with them continues within us as long as we live." Charles Taylor, *Philosophical Arguments* (Cambridge, MA: Harvard University Press, 1993), 230.

[7] Francis A. Schaeffer, *The Complete Works of Francis A. Schaeffer: A Christian Worldview* (Wheaton, IL: Crossway Books, 1982), Vol. 1, 288–91.

naturalistic universe. Biblical narratives do not inform Christian interpretations as they once did in Western culture.[8]

Even if a person attempts to claim his or her identity without regard to God, family, and culture, most people still give some degree of authority to an outside voice to tell them who they are. We search for glory and meaning. Whether it is positive or negative, true or false, our default mode is to misplace our trust in some other source of authority to tell us who we are. We simply cannot escape the question of authority or avoid living without an answer. *Who have you given the authority to tell your identity?*

It is clear that the gospel accounts take the early chapters to clarify Jesus's identity before He reached approximately thirty years old. What was He doing in a carpenter shop for thirty years? One thing is certain: Jesus of Nazareth received a strong, foundational, and clear sense of identity before entering fully into calling. The opening chapters of Matthew and Luke record His genealogy, John the Baptist's identification of Jesus, His birth narrative, and the Father's affirming identity-voice from heaven at His baptism. Jesus is the Messiah (the Christ). He is the Father's beloved Son in whom His Father is well-pleased. In the same way, we may receive a solid sense of self, place, purpose, and story because Christians have been united with Him. Our identities are, therefore, given to each us in Christ.

---

[8] Taylor writes: "The rise of the buffered identity has been accompanied by an interiorization; that is, not only the Inner/Outer distinction, that between Mind and World as separate loci, which is central to the buffer itself; and not only the development of this Inner/Outer distinction in a whole range of epistemological theories of a mediational type from Descartes to Rorty;' but also the growth of a rich vocabulary of interiority, an inner realm of thought and feeling to be explored. This frontier of self-exploration has grown, through various spiritual disciplines of self-examination, through Montaigne, the development of the modern novel, the rise of Romanticism, the ethic of authenticity, to the point where we now conceive of ourselves as having inner depths." See Charles Taylor, *A Secular Age*, 238–39.

Why this focus on identity in the early years of His life? Why is the length of thirty years spent on His identity up to the point of His baptism? It is because Jesus would now enter the next season of His life—namely His calling. These early, strengthening affirmations of His identity prepared Him for the interpretation war that followed in the wilderness against Satan's lies and throughout His life. If Satan could dismantle Jesus's identity beforehand, then he could sabotage His calling. Therefore, a solid sense of one's identity in Christ ought to precede living out one's calling to Christ.

How much more do Christians need a strong sense of identity in Christ! Before we rush off in our callings when we are young adults, even daily throughout our lives, we must ask ourselves: does the gospel shape my identity? What material is God using in your identity-formation process from the genesis of your story? Let's discover the reason why your identity in Christ must begin at the beginning of the gospel (creation) and include your past and family (providence). We'll begin with providence and then how God made us (creation). God has been providentially using your genealogy, name, ethnicity, and place or culture to shape you into the likeness of Christ.

Providence: An Antidote to Radical Individualism

No one has simply been hurled into the kingdom of God without a past, without a story and an Author, and without a meaningful and purposeful existence within the context of a family, heritage, and ethnicity.

Besides God's work of creating all things and peoples, God has been sustaining and governing all things toward one great aim— namely, His own glory and our joy. This is what I mean by providence. We are not radical individuals, separated from our families of origin or by adoption. We were conceived in our mother's womb, in a family, and marked by previous generations. In the ancient world, one's genealogy was like one's resume, listing one's credentials, as it were. Jesus's genealogy included the good, the bad, and the ugly of significant people, places, and ethnicities that mattered and had weight on his identity. Their names are in relation to Jesus's name and therefore remembered. The names tell the family stories in God's providence, often in relation to the narrative of redemptive history. For example, Abraham means "father of many." Isaac, born to his parents in their old age, means "laughter."

Their names and lives tell identity stories, and all their stories are connected to the gospel story and narrative at large—God's providence is recorded in the historically reliable acts of God's redemptive work throughout the generations of humanity with settings, characters, and a plot. The plot is a purposeful arrangement of events with a beginning, a middle, and an end. It has tension leading to resolution in Jesus Christ as the Savior of humanity. The Bible develops from innocence to fall and from redemption to consummation.

You have an identity given to you by God. Any sense of autonomous claim or right to define or name oneself is to let evil or others claim that ultimate place of authority that only God should have. These must be renounced. God ordained your family to name you, whatever the motives your parents had. God fashioned and shaped you in your mother's womb, and He has sustained your ethnicity with pleasure and gladly chose your gender with intentional pleasure and wisdom.

God did two major works in carrying out His eternal decrees: the work of creation and the work of providence. After He created all things, He has been sustaining and governing all things for His own glory. In God's sustaining and ruling all things with redemptive purpose in each of our lives, it came to pass that we were each born, and we were given a name in a family context with an ethnicity and a genealogy. Once you appreciate God's work of providence, like Joseph in Genesis 50, then you will own who you are in His larger global purposes for His name and glory.

Providence is the gift your heart was made to want, which gave you a sense of being authored and enjoying the Author's perspective (an authority to trust while interpreting its meaningful plot). Plot elevates *chronos* (time as we know it) to the felt level of *kairos* (story time).[9] Your story is God's story, and the tension of His plot is felt in the suffering, longings, and struggling for God to resolve them. What is your heart's quest, which your inner self longs to surmount but requires you to trust God for? How does evil tempt you to escape the tension of waiting on God in faith? God gave you a story with a plot, an evil enemy, and a happy consummation to envision. However ordinary your life's story may appear, I believe you will know within that it has transcendence and meaning for a larger story with eternal consequences.

Your Story

Before you were named, you were. Psalm 139:15–16 honors God as the author of our individual story by mentioning His "book." He who knew you before you were made, knew you and knitted you together before you were born in your mother's womb. To know your story is to know how God has shaped you into a new creation in Christ with a past, a present, and a future.[10] Your story has a

---

[9] *Kairos* (καιρός) is an ancient Greek word meaning the right or opportune moment (the supreme moment). The ancient Greeks had two words for time: *chronos* and *kairos*. While the former refers to chronological or sequential time, the latter signifies a time lapse, a moment of indeterminate time in which everything happens.

[10] See Dan B. Allender, *To Be Told* (Colorado Springs, CO: Waterbrook Press, 2005).

redemptive plot. The tension of this plot weaves themes until it is resolved through owning your true identity in Christ, fulfilling your God-given destiny, and overcoming regret and busyness with intentionality, until a glorious resolution of grace prevails from your gospel legacy. Leaving a gospel blessing with one arm stretched out over the next generation and another reaching for the upward prize as you are crossing the river of death and receiving the festal shout of heaven's welcome. Your life story, and a clear identity in Christ, is what matters most.

Your Name

When we name something or someone, it means that we steward it or a person. Adam and Eve named the kinds of created plants and animals and each other. On the one hand, they could not exploit or abuse creation. On the other hand, they could not neglect creation or their family with passive laziness. They were stewards of God's world. People name their pets and things they own as stewards of them. Parents are given stewardship of their children to raise them and send them off into their callings. They do not own their children; God owns all.

Christian names are outward expressions of what people are inwardly good at being, doing, and demonstrating. When Adam named the first woman Eve (Life-giver), he had the power to peer into her glory and to draw out her calling. To this day, a spouse's voice trumps all other voices with the authority to enhance or to degrade. Jesus perceived Simon (Pebble) had a greater heart and glory than his outward name expressed. So Jesus renamed him Peter (Rock). Saul (big man) had a Christian name of Paul (little man), which expressed the glory of humility in Christ.

What is your given name, your full name, and why were you given those names? What do your first, last, and middle names literally express by way of family meaning? For example, many people are named by their parent(s) after another family relative or culturally important person. Whatever your name is, it has shaped you in some way. How does the gospel rule you through your name when you hear or speak it?

Who had authority to name Jesus? His parents did not, because God the Father told Joseph to name his son *Jesus* to express that His glory was like the name *Joshua* (renamed by Moses from *Hosea*), which meant He will save His people. Jesus is not stewarded. He only names others, us. He has named the Christian with a new name to be revealed in heaven. In the book of Genesis, God renamed Abraham and Jacob, yet their birth names were meaningful to God's narrative and their testimony to future generations. Joseph called the name of the firstborn Manasseh. "For," he said, "God has made me forget all my hardship and all my father's house." The name of the second he called Ephraim, "For God made me fruitful in the land of my affliction" (Genesis 41:51–52). These two names tell the gospel story and about God's providence in Joseph's lifetime after being mistreated in childhood and suffering in Egypt. Can you research your names a bit? Perhaps a parent or older sibling can help you understand your family context and story.

The Bible makes much of your name. No matter what great works you perform (or do not), your name is great, and it is written in heaven. As you overcome evil and the challenges of the Christian life, you are promised the delightful discovery of God's new name given just for you.[11]

---

[11] See Luke 10:20; Revelation 13:18.

Your Ethnicity

What is your ethnicity? Every parent wants his or her child to embrace the family's ethnicity, but this can be challenging today. A Chinese-American mother and white American husband of English-Dutch-Irish descent have two children. Although their five-year-old son knows his maternal grandparents were born in China and that his mom speaks Cantonese sometimes, he said to his mother with certainty: "*You're* Chinese, but I'm not." Bonnie Tsui, the mother of the boy, concluded: "Much as I hate to admit it, what they choose to be won't necessarily have to do with me. Because my sons are going to be the ones who say who—not *what*—they are."[12]

Contemporary culture leaves the answer to this difficult question of identity to the individual. Since the ethnic, and sometimes gender, question of identity is too much for agreement and consensus between generations and ethnic groups, it is left to the individual. Nevertheless, your ethnicity and culture matter. Americans often don't know they have a culture until they enter another culture. We all have a culture and a cultural identity, and ethnicity plays an important role.[13] Have you traced your genealogy back a few generations to discover how your identity has been shaped by past generations? After listening to hundreds of Christians share their identities in Christ (using the template in the conclusion) among campus staff, pastors, seminary students, and church members, it is astounding how much inner strength is given to a Christian by

---

[12] Bonnie Tsui, "Choose Your Own Identity," *The New York Times Magazine* (December 14, 2015). http://www.nytimes.com/2015/12/14/magazine/choose-your-own-identity. Tsui is the author of *American Chinatown: A People's History of Five Neighborhoods* (New York, NY: Free Press, 2009).

[13] Romanian historian and philosopher Mircea Eliade has sought to address the nature of how are ethnic, religious, and culture influences our sense of identity in *A History of Religious Ideas* (Chicago, IL: The University of Chicago Press, 1982), 3 Vols.

simply embracing his or her names, stories, and cultural ethnicities that God has given him or her!

Some people, however, struggle to renounce the lies of what other cultural and ethnic groups say of their particular people group or ethnicity, but this must be done.[14] No one has that authority, however, except the Creator and Redeemer of all peoples; namely, Christ Jesus. Jesus's genealogy embraces both Jews and outsiders from Moab, Hittite, Canaanite, and other ethnic and cultural people groups.

Jesus models and teaches the inclusion of outsiders and not to exclude the "sinners." If we idolize our group (e.g., our nation, race, class, generation, sub culture, or people of the same gender or marital status), we invariably demonize those unlike us. One Christian author believes:

> This simple concept explains the "isms" of our world (nationalism, racism, classism, sexism, ageism, etc.). This also explains why most religions and spiritualities are tribal—their god is for them and against people unlike them. Their enemies have the same idolatry but a different deity … This only perpetuates identity idolatry. Even worse, many churches are so deep in their identity idolatry that they're homogeneous not by intention but by lack of intention. They simply don't think of racial and cultural reconciliation.[15]

---

[14] For example, see Orlando Crespo, *Being Latino in Christ: Finding Wholeness in Your Ethnic Identity* (Downers Grove, IL: InterVarsity Press, 2003).

[15] Mark Driscoll, *Who Do You Think You Are?: Finding Your True Identity in Christ* (Nashville, TN: Thomas Nelson, 2013), 84, 86.

Your Heritage: the Good, the Bad, and the Ugly

In the ancient world, one's genealogy was one's resume or curriculum vitae for others to be impressed with one's identity. Often relatives were left out who would be perceived in an unfavorable light. Jesus, however, intentionally included individuals, especially in Matthew's gospel, who were from the wrong side of town, you might say. Matthew's gospel opens with the mention of Jesus's humanity and deity. His relatives listed were noble but also known for family incest, adultery, prostitution, and murder. Although Jesus was Jewish, he had Gentiles in his family line. How does this speak of God's grace and redemption? How does your genealogy tell the gospel?

As you own your story, names, ethnicity, culture, and heritage, you will be more ready to hear and believe the gospel. When you let the gospel rule and answer the question about who you are, you will practice resting in your true identity in Christ. The gospel, however, does not begin with your brokenness or sinfulness as when you first became aware go God's grace in His providence. It begins with your glory. Just as the Bible and the gospel begin in the first chapters of Genesis, so a priority of order in embracing your identity takes us back to first things. You are both unique, and you are an image of God Himself like everyone else.

"I Am the Image of God"

In Genesis 1:26–28 God expressed his intentionality with regard to people: "Let us make man, male and female, in our image." He intended for humanity to bear His image, every human being. Each of us matters. You have a unique thumbprint to identify who you really are. Your presence and being matters because God matters, and you are made in His image. If you were absent, we would all miss you being with us. Everyone bears a glory, which has not ever been erased by the Fall or the Flood or by the abusive speech of others (Genesis 9:6; Psalm 8:5, 139:14; James 3:9).

You are the image of God as the Dutch theologian, Herman Bavinck, wrote:

> The entire world is a revelation of God, a mirror of his virtues and perfections; every creature is in his own way and according to his own measurement an embodiment of a divine thought. But among all creatures only man is the image of God, the highest and richest revelation of God, and therefore head and crown of the entire creation.[16]

God has identified each of us with Himself, and we all have a weighty sense of God's glory. Our longings are never satisfied, for we may conclude that we were built for God and for the new earth. In fact, you and I *are*, we *are*, the image of God. Bavinck's biblical conclusion is clear about this:

> From the doctrine that man has been created in the image of God flows the clear implication that the image extends to man in his entirety. Nothing in man is excluded from the image of God. All creatures reveal traces of God, but only man is the image of God. And he is that image totally, in soul and body, in all conditions and relationships. Man is the image of God because and insofar as he is true man, and he is man, true and real man, because and insofar as he is the image of God.[17]

---

[16] Herman Bavinck, *Reformed Dogmatics* (Grand Rapids, MI: Baker Academic, 2004), Vol. 2, 530–31.

[17] Ibid., 555.

Although we are glorious, we are only an image. We are not God. Besides being in His image, we are also a broken image of God. Since the fall of humanity in the third chapter of Genesis, we are fallen image bearers. Although the image of God remains our identity after the fall, we are all marred images of God. In the words of C. S. Lewis, we are "glorious ruins." We all have glory, and our longings tell us we were made for God and a better place. Nothing in this life fully satisfies because we have too much of a sense of glory, being in God's image. Yet, we are ruined by the fall and in need of redemption.

This means that every person we meet has something quite extraordinary about him or her, including you and your neighbors. There are no ordinary people in your life. C. S. Lewis wrote about it this way:

> It is in the light of these overwhelming possibilities, it is with the awe and the circumspection proper to them, that we should conduct all our dealings with one another, all friendships, all loves, all play, all politics. There are no ordinary people. You have never talked to a mere mortal. Nations, cultures, arts, and civilization—these are mortal, and their life is to ours as the life of a gnat. But it is immortals whom we joke with, work with, marry, snub, and exploit—immortal horrors or ever-lasting splendors. ... Next to the blessed Sacrament itself [communion], your neighbor is the holiest object presented to your senses.[18]

In this famous sermon entitled "The Weight of Glory," Lewis

---

[18] C. S. Lewis, *The Weight of Glory: And Other Addresses* (New York: HarperOne, 2001), 45.

concluded his remarks with one of the most important statements ever uttered about the importance of people and the influence our conduct has upon them. As he pointed out, it is a very serious thing to live in society with other people whose eternal destiny hangs in the balance. Everybody one day will be either glorified or damned by God. We are encouraging them to one of these two destinations by the way we treat them. What does it mean to love a glorious ruin well when *ruin* seems greater than *glory*?

In the Protestant Reformation, John Calvin, wrote a spiritual formation book to answer this very question. When it is our tendency to make more of the ruin of a person or ourselves, we ought to focus on people's glory as God's image bearers. Although people are "a frightful deformity," yet:

> Whatever man you meet who needs your aid, you have no reason to refuse to help him. Say, 'He is a stranger'; but the Lord has given him a mark that ought to be familiar to you … Say, 'He is contemptible and worthless'; but the Lord shows him to be one to whom he has deigned to give the beauty of his image. Say that he does not deserve even your least effort for his sake; but the image of God, which recommends him to you, is worthy of your giving yourself and all your possessions. Assuredly there is but one way in which to achieve what is not merely difficult but utterly against human nature: to love those who hate us, to repay their evil deeds with benefits, to return blessings for reproaches. It is that we remember not to consider men's evil intention but to look upon the image of God in them, which cancels and effaces their

transgressions, and with its beauty and dignity allures us to love and embrace.[19]

So far we have been embracing our identities as given by another, from outside of ourselves, from God's perspective and God Himself. When we acknowledge that God's sovereignty put us in a family and a generational context with a particular name and ethnicity, we are embracing His providence in a way that helps us interpret ourselves through the gospel lens. Then we examined what it means to be made in God's image, and to admit we are both glorious and broken. We are "glorious ruins." There is more to owning our identities than embracing that we are God's image bearers. We are at the same time of conception given our gender—we are either male or female.

Questions for Group Discussion

1. Who have you given the authority to tell you your identity in the past?
2. How has our contemporary culture made identity formation difficult?
3. What does each of your names mean? Why were you given these names?
4. Can you find out about your parents, grandparents, and great-grandparents are?
5. What is your ethnicity? How has this shaped your identity?
6. What does it mean that you are God's image?

---

[19] John Calvin, *Institutes of The Christian Religion* (Philadelphia, PA: The Westminster Press, 1960), Vol. 1, 696–97.

Chapter 2
Gender Redeemed

"I Am a Man or a Woman."

You are a man, or you are a woman. Femininity or masculinity is irrevocably and inerasably endowed into our being so that nobody is correct in claiming, "I am first a person and then female or male."[20] Our soul has only existed with vitality and potentiality according to the gender God intended for us. I am a man and not a woman. God spoke very intentionally according to the original Hebrew in Genesis 1:26–28: "Let us make man in our image, male (*zakar*) and female (*neqebah*)."

Some parents may no longer answer the question at birth: Is it a boy or a girl? They may answer calmly, "Our child will decide that later and let us all know their answer eventually." American educators tell their students that one's gender is not only a choice,

---

[20] Some Christians argue for another gender category, namely, "intersex." I am not convinced that this category will be redeemed and exist in the new earth. Epigenesists, as well, will further complicate this discussion. Megan K. DeFranza, *Sex Difference in Christian Theology: male, female, and intersex in the image of God* (Grand Rapids, MI: Eerdmans, 2015), 184.

but it is a flexible one. Sexual reassignment by surgery is optional.[21] Nevertheless, the uniqueness of our being male or female reaches to the core of our identities when God genders each of us at conception.

Men, God intended for each of you to be a man and not a woman. Women, God intended for each of you to be female and not male. God differentiated masculinity and femininity to be glorious, different, yet equal in glory. God delights in women and the gender of being female, just as He does for men being masculine. One of our common struggles, however, is that we do not delight in who God made us in the same way He does. A Christian struggling with same-sex attraction came to see me in my office yesterday. He is one of many today who long to live out of their true identities, but long so much for "vitamin M" (masculine affirmation and love) or "vitamin F" (feminine affirmation and love) that it is harder to own their gender calling. Sexual drives complicate accepting gender being and glory, not to mention the ruin of the fall and the gender curses.

What do men and women need to understand about their gender in terms of their glory, fallen nature, and redemption? First, that people are both glorious and fallen; both blessed and cursed. The intention behind the curse on each gender, however, is gracious or redemptive. As the hymn writer says, "Behind a frowning providence He hides a smiling face."[22]

Both genders share a direct correlation between their gender's glory and gender's curse (Genesis 2–3). God is not the Author of evil. It is because of Satan's lie and Adam's sin that people are ruined. It is because God is the giver of all good gifts that we are endowed

---

[21] Megan K. DeFranza seems to go too far in giving the impression that "intersexuals" will be redeemed in Revelation as intersected people. For a better resource, see Larry Crabb, *Men & Women: Enjoying the Difference*, (Grand Rapids, MI: Zondervan, 1991).

[22] William Cowper's hymn, "God Moves in Mysterious Ways His Wonders to Perform," explained at Gospel Coalition website: https://www.thegospelcoalition.org/article/god-moves-in-a-mysterious-way.

with glory, that the glory remains, and that His curse is gracious in a mysterious way. Why is the curse directed at the gender's glory? God has a redemptive aim. Until we admit we are licked, that our autonomous strategies cannot overcome the curse and get us back to Eden, we will never cry out for a Redeemer to save us and transform us into His glorious image again. Dr. Larry Crabb explains:

> God's judgments on both the man and the woman were neither rude nor uncaring. God's intent was to discourage Adam and Eve (and their descendants) from thinking that their lives could ever work without him and to help them realize that the full realization of joy awaits a new heaven and earth. He wanted to hedge them in, to surface a despair that would drive them back to himself.[23]

In one sense, both are true about every Christian. For example, I am a glorious man and a fallen man. In the words of C. S. Lewis in *Prince Caspian*: "You come of the Lord Adam and the Lady Eve, and that's both honor enough to lift up the head of the poorest beggar, and shame enough to bow the shoulders of the greatest emperor on earth."[24] Since I am a Christian, however, I am also a redeemed man. Each new creation in Christ is all three—namely, a redeemed glorious ruin.

Embracing your true identity according to gender, then, requires an understanding of all three aspects of glory, fall, and redemption. First, let's consider what it means to be a Christian male.

---

[23] Larry Crabb, *Men & Women: Enjoying the Difference*, (Grand Rapids, MI: Zondervan, 1991), 150–58.

[24] C. S. Lewis, *Prince Caspian* (New York: HarperTrophy, 1951), 218.

The Glory of Masculinity

What's so glorious about masculinity? In Genesis 2 we read about man made from the dust, working with strength as gardener and guardian of the trees. Males love dirt and are meant in some way when they transform culture through intense labor to make it fruitful, provisional, and beautiful. He names as God's steward and is glorious when he enhances glory without neglecting creation. He is made to tell stories and to remember what matters (*zakar*). He passionately sings poetic and doxological delight over the woman God has given him. He names her in a way that peers into her glory and calls her best into existence. As God ordains the institution of marriage, we see how sons will demonstrate a movement away from parents toward a woman for her welfare and marital oneness. Sons pursue women and multiply their lives, leaving a lasting impression on future generations. In man's physic, men are generally stronger though tender. He is meant to strongly penetrate this world and his wife with tenderness in order to leave a mark (*zakar*) and multiply his fruitful efforts. The glory of masculinity is revealed in Genesis 2.

A man embraces the glory of his identity when he exercises a tender strength to provide and protect, to remember and delight over, and to move toward creation and people in sacrificial love for God's glory. Why is it hard to experience and live this?

The Fallenness of Masculinity

In Genesis 3 we see a picture of fallen manhood. Man is silent, while his wife dialogues with Satan (3:6). He doesn't protect her from the tree but only listens and transgresses. Original righteousness was lost that day. He hides from God in shame and covers it. He shifts the guilt and blame on God and others ever since (3:9–12). The curse on men is directly related to their masculine glory. All his best efforts in the dirt and with the earth bears fruitless thistles and thorns and dehydration. Every man struggles with nihilism, the belief that nothing matters. All his hard work will never satisfy, for every man returns to the dust at death. Every male, boy or adult man, knows he is "not enough," or inadequate (3:17–19).

The Redemption of Masculinity

Tucked away in God's curse of the serpent is the gospel (Genesis 3:15); namely, that another man will come one day and crush Satan's head, rescue the bride, and save us from the curse. He will redeem the creation and rename a new humanity. The grace in the curse is that God will not let masculinity remain in the fallen state. He immediately promised another Adam—namely, Jesus Christ. God also curses masculinity only to the intensity that every man would admit he is licked. Men still provide, work, delight in their wives, and protect the vulnerable. They still marry and have children, but a redeemed man embraces the sorrow that he is not enough without the Savior. He trusts in Christ, and through God's grace in his weakness and insufficiency, he acts out of the glory of his masculine identity knowing that right now there is a calling to fulfill east of Eden that counts for eternity and the new earth. Men, who enjoy a reasonable satisfying awareness of the substance God has placed within a man's being, desire to make an eternal contribution to God's purposes in this world. They trust God, in spite of what is seen or felt, that the mundane, sacrificial way of love counts for eternity.

Every man will struggle to build what will eventually turn to into dust, but trust that God will make all things new and all our labors matter. Often men attempt to escape the sorrow of insignificance by becoming vicariously involved in the suffering of NFL football players trying to gain another ten yards. True manhood, however, engages in suffering to enhance relationship. Then he will enjoy being a wild man engaged in the wildest thing of all—loving well.

A redeemed man faces the thorns and thistles of a fallen world, yet persistently moves forward without giving into futility. We don't give into futility but allow it to break us until we see the value of Christ taking the curse on Himself at the cross. There He paid the price to redeem us and give us the worth and glory we have all been chasing after for years.

The Glory of Femininity

What's so glorious about a woman? Most would agree, "A woman's glory is her beauty." In Genesis 2 we see the glory of a woman. The man is delighting in her beauty. A woman is to be adored, sung over, and fought for. She is made from the rib of the man. In other words, she is gifted relationally. Whereas men are often clueless when it comes to relational awareness, she has an innate sense of the quality of community. She is a helper (*ezer*). God is referred to as our helper (*ezer*) in many passages (Exodus 18:4; Deuteronomy 33:7, 26, 29; Psalm 33:20; 115:9–11; 124:8; 140:5). A woman's glory is her powerful ability to help others. A woman is also tender, usually physically more so than men. She opens her heart to be entered (*neqebah*). In physical appearance, she is meant to open her heart to a godly leader and with tender strength wrap herself around and adjust to her husband's love. She is glorious when she gives birth to, and nurtures, a network of relationships. Her beauty attracts relational movement toward her, and she surrounds those relationships with tender nurture. She is a life-giver (*thelus* Greek), inviting and sustaining life-giving intimacy and care. She displays dignity when she tends to value giving something of her soul to nourish relationships and deepen attachments. Her focus is less on going into the world to make her mark and more on welcoming a community for the sake of enhancing it.

The Fallenness of Femininity

In the fall of the woman (Genesis 3), we observe her desiring to know what she should not (3:5–6). A fallen woman desires to know the gossip beyond the boundaries of safe relational boundaries. Like man, she hides her shame and blames others (3:9–12), but particularly we see a woman's fallenness in the woman's curse. Notice how she is cursed directly in the area of her glory; namely, in her relationships. She has pain in giving birth to relationships (3:13) and desires to control her primary one: her husband (3:16). Every fallen woman is controlling of the people she longs for intimacy from most. If every fallen man is aware he is "not enough," then every fallen woman senses her longing for intimate relationships is "too much." Her desire to have her husband is "too much" for any man, except Jesus. This implies that women have some level of desperation and strong desire inside that often terrifies men's sense of inadequacy to come through for her. Beware of men, who want to shut you down and silence you through shaming or fearful threats. A redeemed woman will not hate her loneliness or frenetically attempt to fill it by cleaning the house four more times.

The Redemption of Femininity

There is a Redeemer promised to come to remove the curse and crush the serpent's head (Genesis 3:15). He delights over the woman, even the church (Ephesians 5), and brings her to the wedding feast in the new earth (Revelation 21). A redeemed woman, who embraces Christ as her Savior is free to face the fall and long for the wedding day. She embraces the sorrow of her unmet longings in a way that shows she has repented of her entitlements to ideal relations. She doesn't give into her loneliness but allows herself to be broken by it and redeemed from it. She opens her heart and encircles others for the sake of gospel nurturing (Titus 2), knowing there is an eternal weight of glory that her relational contractions are giving birth to. Though the reality of her own wretchedness and frustration in primary relationships is excruciating, she trusts God for her deepest longings. She is sufficient in Christ to stand with her arms outstretched, beckoning others to life in Christ. When she embraces the gospel, she begins to attract others to hope that glory will be fully restored through the second Adam—namely, Christ.

Femininity, at its core, is most at rest when women consciously enjoy the weight of glory God has placed within their being, which is clearly evident in their desire and longing for intimate relationships. When a woman trusts God's favor on her through Christ, she is enabled to confidently and warmly invite others to life through her relationship with God and herself.

There are a thousand ways women attempt to escape their loneliness and to invite others' suffering. God, however, invites women into their own suffering so they may rediscover where they lost their voice along the way. A redeemed woman clarifies her desire and sense of calling by facing her pain and loneliness with the gospel, for her service without desire is deadening. A redeemed woman calls forth the good in her husband, others, and herself in order to discover how delightful she was meant to be, while giving others a taste of God's goodness. She is willing to be lonely, knowing heartbreak, while keeping her heart open and tender in her milieu of relationships.[25]

---

[25] If a man or woman is not married, they should know that they are not "cursed" or unloved. Rather, as Paul states in 1 Corinthians 7, is just as glorious and redeemed in being single. Our text in Genesis 2-3 speaks of marriage, but how wonderful our gender relates to being single!

Same-Sex Strugglers

There are three challenges for the church to face in our time: (1) the conflict between sexual and Christian identity. (2) The developmental process of identity formation. (3) Competing perspectives from the mainstream of the gay community and from local churches. Mark A. Yarhouse believes that there is "the Gay identity script," which asserts that same-sex attractions reflect real differences between people, not just behavioral choices, but that these attractions determine your identity, and that your attractions reside in the core of your identity. Therefore, if you are "gay," then you follow through. This script is based on the two assumptions that one is either born gay or not, and to not act out of one's same-sex sexual drive is to deny one's identity.[26]

The gospel narrative is counter to this. The biblical script states that same-sex attractions are a result of the fall, that same-sex attraction may be an important part of your experience, that acting on same-sex attractions is separate from your identity, and that there is hope to enjoy life without acting on same-sex attractions.

People were very responsive to Bruce (Caitlyn) Jenner, who was in some ways applauded for his self-definition when he announced a name in 2015 saying: "I am Cait." This is a reflection of our contemporary struggle with our individual identities, along with statistics that 40 percent of transgender youth have committed suicide. In April 2015 Bruce Jenner was selected as one of Barbara Walter's most of ten most influential persons of the year.

Bruce Jenner's headline-grabbing transformation into "Caitlyn" has captured our society's attention. Whether Christians or theologians are ready or not, questions about how sexual identity is formed are now inescapable.

---

[26] Mark A. Yarhouse, *Understanding Sexual Identity: A Resource for Youth Ministry* (Grand Rapids, MI: Zondervan, 2013), 70.

The wisdom of this age is always dated. In ancient Rome, Fernando of Pompeii had a statue of himself as a woman. In the 1970s, students were told in school that gender not fixed or genetic, but in 2015, cultural authorities seem to be saying you are a male or a female unless you manipulate it.

How should we respond to those who don't seem to have been created male or female? But what about those who are "intersex"—born with bodily or biological conditions that blur the physical line between male and female? Having no such celebrity figurehead, they have received considerably less attention, even within the conservative evangelical world.

In "Sex Difference" in *Christian Theology: Male, Female, and Intersex in the Image of God*, theologian Megan DeFranza attempts to fill this gap. The book provides a robust theological framework that "makes space" for intersex individuals while holding on to core evangelical commitments. DeFranza is right that conservative evangelicals need to attend closely to the ways intersex individuals might challenge traditional "gender binaries" between male and female. Her book, however, leads into a tangled theological thicket, without suggesting a workable path forward.[27]

---

[27] DeFranza's book is divided into two sections. In the first, she outlines how the medicalizing of our bodies made "intersex" conditions invisible to our contemporary Western consciousness. She then plumbs Jesus's claim that "some are born eunuchs" (Matt. 19:12), suggesting that the Bible contains resources for recognizing those who do not fit the standard understanding of male and female. And she provides a hasty overview of how we ostensibly went from one sex (male) in the classical period, to two in modernity (male and female), to the postmodern proliferation of sexes. (One theorist proposes five sexes, while another suggests hundreds.)

Putting It All Together

The first stage of understanding our identities is to embrace our original design and family history. God created us to be His image bearers. According to His providence, we were placed in a family, who named and raised us within an ethnic culture. Since He also created us either male or female to uniquely reflect God's glory, it helps to embrace the threefold aspect of each gender. Christians must come to terms with both their gender glory and ruin in order to truly embrace their identities as a redeemed man or woman.

Although a Christian is redeemed, his or her default mode is still set on autonomy—to assume we can live life without God's grace. Though everyone lost original righteousness in the first man (Adam), in the perfect Man (the second Adam) God declares the ungodly (both genders) righteousness in His sight (justification). The gospel covers our shame and loneliness (adoption), and it transforms our former tendency to withdraw from God's presence (sanctification). Although many Christians acknowledge these truths in their heads, they live in a functionally autonomous way, somewhat defeated in *the* interpretation war over Christian identity. The interpretation war for our identities is the subject of the next chapter.

Questions for Group Discussion

1. What is so glorious about men?
2. What is so glorious about women?
3. What is fallen about men?
4. What is fallen about women?
5. How are you glorious?
6. How are you fallen?
7. What does a redeemed man look and act like?
8. What does a redeemed woman look and act like?

Chapter 3

The Interpretation War

The Interpretation War

An interpretation war has existed since the time the ancient serpent tempted Adam and Eve in the garden of Eden. After the fall, this interpretation war grew much more complex as people did not turn to God for meaning and answers to life's basic questions. There is a real battle that rages in the heart of every Christian. It is an interpretation war about his or her identity. This is where the world and the devil seek to kill, steal, and destroy us. This is where the interpretation war takes place each and every day. It is believed that the Reformer Martin Luther said,

> If I profess, with the loudest voice and the clearest exposition, every portion of the truth of God except precisely that little point which the world and the devil are at that moment attacking, I am not confessing Christ, however boldly I may be professing Christianity. Where the battle rages the loyalty of the soldier is proved; and to be steady on

all the battle-field besides is mere flight and disgrace
to him if he flinches at that one point.[28]

Where the Christian soldier is proved is what he or she believes
about his or her identity. Just as Satan attacked Jesus's identity first,
so evil seeks to attack who we *are* before harassing what we *do*.
Have you ever pondered why Christians seem to struggle more with
condemnation than nonbelievers? Before conversion most people
feel all right about who they are, but after conversion, the Christian
is awakened to the law and the accuser. Christians often live with a
great degree of condemning thoughts about who they are, and it is
helpful to identify one central condemning thought.

One's central condemning thought (CCT) is furnished readily by
evil to interpret painful events in our lives. It offers an explanation for
why there was relational damage, and it can trigger an autonomous
vow to never let it happen again. An identity built on a condemning
thought can rule a Christian for many years, instead of the gospel.
This is because our default mode is to overcome condemnation by
self-improvement efforts to prove the lie is a lie. One's CCT triggers
a personal strategy of Christian performance that leads to patterns
of burnout, surrender, and repeat performances. Why are we so
vulnerable to this?

Simply put: we tend to base our sense of our identities upon our
Christian performance, rather than resting on the performance
of another—namely, Jesus Christ's perfect thirty-three-year life
of righteousness. Rather than starting our day off secure in our
position in Christ, we rush off to perform for what we already have
on the front end. After we perform well, we think it was a good thing
we prayed and read the Bible that morning.

---

[28] Martin Luther quoted by Francis Schaeffer in *The Great Evangelical Disaster*
(Wheaton, IL: Crossway Books, 1984), 50–51.

The Nature and Function of Deceit

And Jesus, full of the Holy Spirit, returned from the Jordan and was led by the Spirit in the wilderness for forty days, being tempted by the devil. And he ate nothing during those days. And when they were ended, he was hungry. The devil said to him, "If you are the Son of God, command this stone to become bread." And Jesus answered him, "It is written, 'Man shall not live by bread alone.'" And the devil took him up and showed him all the kingdoms of the world in a moment of time, and said to him, "To you I will give all this authority and their glory, for it has been delivered to me, and I give it to whom I will. If you, then, will worship me, it will all be yours." And Jesus answered him, "It is written, 'You shall worship the Lord your God, and him only shall you serve.'" And he took him to Jerusalem and set him on the pinnacle of the temple and said to him, "If you are the Son of God, throw yourself down from here, for it is written, 'He will command his angels concerning you, to guard you,' and 'On their hands they will bear you up, lest you strike your foot against a stone.'" And Jesus answered him, "It is said, 'You shall not put the Lord your God to the test.'" And when the devil had ended every temptation, he departed from him until an opportune time. (Luke 4:1–13)

The Timing of Deceit

Noticing the timing and the identity-directed aim of Satan's strategies reveals the nature and function of deceit. First observe the timing of deceit. Satan strikes when Jesus is most vulnerable. Children are excellent observers but poor interpreters. Many children believe lies from the evil one and need a parent to interpret life according to the gospel. When we are hungry and overtired, lonely and weak, evil seeks to destroy us by attacking our identities. It was "an opportune time," and Satan departs Jesus for another time when Jesus will be vulnerable to the deception. When are you usually attacked?

The Aim of Deceit

Satan aims directly at Jesus's identity, not his performance. Satan says two times, "*if* you are the Son of God" and is tempted to lose His identity by worshiping Satan. The Father had just told Jesus at His baptism, "You are my beloved Son in whom I am well pleased," and Satan's arrow shoots right for that target. Why? Because if Satan can destroy Christ's identity, he could ruin everything else that follows. The Christian, too, must stand firm and remember who he or she is in Christ. Bryan Chapell illustrates Satan's aim, and how we need the gospel. He wrote:

> As I was pastoring the rural church attended by farmers and coal miners—people accustomed to hard lives—I heard a story that taught me more about the nature and foundation of true faith than I had gained in much of my seminary education. The story tells of a miner who, though a stalwart believer, was injured at a young age. He became an invalid. Over the years he watched through

a window near his bed as life passed him by. He watched fellow workers marry, raise families, and have grandchildren. He watched the company he had served thrive without attempting to make adequate provision for his loss. He watched as his body withered, his house crumbled, and hope for better things in this life died.

Then, one day when the bedridden miner was quite old, a younger man came to visit him. "I hear that you believe in God and claim that he loves you," said the young man. "How can you believe such things after all that has happened to you?"

The old man hesitated and then smiled. He said, "Yes, there are days of doubt. Sometimes Satan comes calling on me in this fallen-down old house of mine. He sits right there by my bed, where you are sitting now. He points out my window to the men I once worked with whose bodies are still strong, and Satan asks, 'Does Jesus love you?' Then, Satan makes me look at my tattered room as he points to the fine homes of my friends and asks again, 'Does Jesus love you?' Finally, Satan points to the grandchild of a friend of mine—a man who has everything I do not—and Satan waits for the tear in my eye before he whispers in my ear, 'Does Jesus really love you?'"

Startled by the candor of the old man's responses, the younger man asked, "And what do you say when Satan speaks to you that way?"

Said the old miner, "I take Satan by the hand, and I lead him to a hill far away called Calvary. There I point to the nail-pierced hands, the thorn-torn brow, and the spear-pierced side. Then I say to Satan, 'Doesn't Jesus love me!'"[29]

The Power and Authority of Identity

Unlike Jesus, we have believed a lie about who we each are. At vulnerable moments and opportune times, Satan shot his arrows into our inmost beings. These lies and condemning thoughts about our identities feel so true in the moment that we embrace them and unwittingly let them rule us. These lies interpret life for us and offer an explanation for pain.

Taking the Central Condemning Thought (CCT) or Core Lie Captive

Before we know it, they function for us. Once a core lie is embedded in a person's soul, he or she will begin to try to overcome it. Since it is negative and condemning, it is natural for a person to attempt to try to prove it wrong. We each want an identity that is better, certainly not a dreadful one. Ask God to let you become aware of your central condemning thought or core lie. Here are common lies or core fears, which whole personalities profiles have been developed from a pathological point of view:

1. I am corrupt, evil, or defective.
2. I am unworthy of being loved.

---

[29] Bryan Chapell, *The Hardest Sermons You'll Ever Have to Preach* (Grand Rapids, MI: Zondervan, 2011), 14–15.

3. I am worthless.
4. I am unknown and personally insignificant.
5. I am useless, helpless, and incapable.
6. I am without support and guidance.
7. I am deprived and hurting.
8. I am a victim and controlled by others.
9. I am voiceless and anxious.[30]

Once a Christian can identify a core lie, basic fear, or central condemning thought, then that person is in a position to identify the foolish strategies he or she has come up with to overcome the lie. For example, my lie is that I am unknown and personally insignificant. The foolish strategies I have autonomously come up with (my default mode) must also be exposed in order to make certain that only the gospel is ruling my life.

Exposing Foolish Strategies

Most of my foolish strategies have been to perform well in Christian ways so I will never be abandoned or left out. The problem is they don't work and are not motivated by loving others well. Eventually, someone does dismiss me or relationally moves on away from me no matter how hard I try. This only reinforces the lie, and I often swing over and surrender to the lie. "You see," I say to myself. "It's true. I am unwanted as personally significant or worth being known." This cycle reinforces one's core fear and leads to burnout, self-hatred, and even depression. Have you ever surrendered to Satan's lie?

What's worse is that a lot of Christians are performing many Christian duties for the wrong reasons. Rather than being free to

---

[30] Enneagram Personality Profiles can offer helpful tools but often promote other worldviews that are not gospel-oriented. For a gospel use of this, see Beth McCord's helpful blog: yourenneagramcoach.com.

love others well out of their gospel identities, they are focused on overcoming their condemning thoughts, which is self-centered. The hilarious thing about this is that it is a fool's errand, a waste of energy. Attempting to obtain an identity we *already* have in Christ on the front end is surely foolish. Thus, they are foolish strategies.

How Our Central Condemning Thought (CCT) Can Misinterpret

There is an added pathological consequence that happens when people are embracing their false identities marked by condemnation, which is that we tend to *project* our lies onto others. We think others are thinking of us according to Satan's condemning identity. We project onto others that they think we are unwanted, worthless, failures, etc. Can you imagine how much of this may be happening in a community when many project their false identities on others all at once? The father of lies could have a heyday. Here is how two writers, Timothy S. Lane and Paul David Tripp, describe the pathology of finding our identities in anyone other than Christ:

> If I am seeking to get identity from you, I will watch you too closely, listen to you too intently, and need you too fundamentally. I will ride the roller coaster of your best and worst moments and everything in between. And because I am watching you too closely, I will become acutely aware of your weaknesses and failures. I will become overly critical, frustrated, disappointed, hopeless, and angry. I will be angry not because you are a sinner but because you have failed to deliver the one thing I seek from you: identity. But none of us will ever get the well being that comes from knowing who we are

from our relationships. Instead we will be left with
damaged relationships filled with hurt, frustration
and anger.[31]

You would think that simply learning about how we function
out of Satan's lies, our CCTs, and coming up with foolish strategies,
would solve our relational messes. We all wish it was that easy,
but the surprising truth is that spiritual formation is a process of
exercising gospel strength on a much more daily fashion.

Cherishing Our CCT (Central Condemning Thought)

When I counsel Christians and they are able to name their central
condemning thoughts or core lies that the evil one bombards them
with on a regular basis, I always ask, "Would you like to renounce
it as a lie?" Do you know how people commonly respond? "Sure,"
they'll say. That's when I upset them a bit because I respond, "I don't
think so. I believe you cherish your lie. I believe it has functioned
for you for a long time." It is surprising to me how I find it so easy to
embrace my lie after all these years.

We will never renounce a central condemning thought about
our identities until we see how it has functioned for us to get what
we wanted from others, which to some degree functioned for us to
make us feel better about ourselves. It is essential that the Christians
see how these strategies only lead to disappointment and to help
them get fed up and sick of them altogether. Repentance of a lie that
has been ruling you is one thing, but for repentance to bear fruit,
it requires the renunciation of the foolish strategies that went along
with it. Can you see how your false identity functioned for you and

---

[31] Timothy S. Lane and Paul David Tripp, *Relationships: A Mess Worth Making*
(Greensboro, NC: New Growth Press), 60.

may be hard to give up until you are fed up with it? Can you identify your foolish strategies to prove you are not what evil says of you?

My Daughter's Story

My daughter, Lizzy, was the ideal pastor's daughter. She and her twin brother were close all their lives (they are the youngest of five). She was the cute, blond cheerleader for her brother on the varsity basketball court and the Christian counselor for the family. She earned perfect grades and caused Karen and me absolutely no trouble (only smiles). Lizzy was born again early in life, and I loved taking her on dates.

Every dark, cold February in central Illinois when school dragged along, I would pick her up early from classes and drive her to Chicago for a dinner and a play. One afternoon as we were on the highway, I was sharing with her about my core lie that I am unknown and perfectly insignificant. She was shocked, since the converse seemed true. It feels so true, however, as we each know. When I was done sharing how I tried to prove it wasn't true with my foolish strategies and how I surrendered to it from time to time, I told her about renouncing the lie and my foolish strategies. I described the benefits of resting in my true identity—namely, less of a roller-coaster Christian experience with more focus on loving others well.

Behind my willingness to share this with Lizzy was my preference. I would rather have a daughter saturated by the gospel and resting within more than a good daughter that made me look good as a pastor. I asked her if she wanted to ask the Lord in prayer what her core lie was—what was the central condemning thought that hummed in her conscience daily. We asked the Holy Spirit to spell it out for us. Big elephant tears began to roll down her beautiful face. "Did He tell you?" I asked. I have always found that the Holy Spirit is more than willing to set us free from our lies and condemning thoughts by the way. She said, "Yes, it is that I am not a good enough girl. I am worthless."

"Not good enough! Worthless? Lizzy," I replied, "everyone one knows that is just not true."

When I asked her if she believed this was from God or Satan, she knew it was from evil. When I asked if she was willing to renounce the lie that she was worthless, since her worth is seen when we see Christ crucified on the cross to redeem her, she said what everyone says. She said yes. That's when her countenance changed, because I said, "I don't think so." Now she was a bit angry with me.

"Lizzy," I said, "I believe you cherish that lie and central condemning thought, because it has functioned for you for years."

She was able to identify her foolish strategies to be good enough and to gain worth. She explained how hard it was to get even a low A grade on a test. She understood more and more as she described the stress she felt to try to prove her worth through perfect relationships, grades, behavior, and Christian duties. She also explained her occasional surrender to the lie and melancholy moods for short seasons.

"Lizzy," I said as her father, "repentance for you would be to get a B-letter grade."

It is not that I am against performing well in our Christian callings, but I prefer for disciples do so for the right reasons and out of their true identities in Christ. Well, Lizzy truly wanted to renounce the lie and her foolish strategies. First, they didn't work. Second, she was on her way to a crash in life. As she renounced the lie and her foolish strategies during that car ride, Satan lost again. Lizzy and I preached the gospel to her soul. Lizzy learned to renounce the lie and not obey the inner impulses to prove her lie was a lie on a daily basis, but she also learned to own her story, the glory as a woman made in God's image, who was justified, adopted, and a saint (more on this in the chapters that follow).

Lizzy graduated as valedictorian of her class, and her speech was not a humanist mantra like, "You're the best class ever, and you can change the world!" Rather, Lizzy preached the gospel to faculty, students, parents, and community. When she finished, the congregation stood on their feet, clapping in praise and glory to Christ for a long time. Obviously, she still earned perfect grades, but she performed out of her identity in Christ and not out of a lie that she was not good enough and worthless.

Winning the War with the Truth of the Gospel

The beauty of the gospel is that we do not have to let evil's lies rule us any more, however true they seem to be. Jesus has lived and been for us the person and life we could never be or live. He has given us our identities based on His performance, and then He paid the penalty for our fallen identities and imperfect performances. We have acceptance on the front end, which motivates us to love others and obey God for the right reasons. Timothy Keller of Redeemer Presbyterian Church in NYC has clarified the operating principle of the gospel well. He wrote:

> There is a great gulf between the understanding that God accepts us because of our efforts and the understanding that God accepts us because of what Jesus has done. Religion operates on the principle, "I obey—therefore I am accepted by God." But the operating principle of the gospel is "I am accepted by God through what Christ has done—therefore I obey."[32]

---

[32] Timothy Keller, *The Reason for God* (New York: Dutton, 2008), 179–80.

The key is embracing the gospel on the front end, then to live out of our true identities in Christ and not vice versa.

Dr. Martyn Lloyd-Jones, a gospel preacher from the previous century, put it this way:

> Here is something, which is truly important, and something which is basic and fundamental to the whole Christian position. The order in which these things are put is absolutely vital. The Apostle does not ask us to do anything until he has first of all emphasized and repeated what God has done for us in Christ. How often have men given the impression that to be Christian means that you display in your life a kind of general belief of faith, and then you add to it virtue and knowledge and charity! To them the Christian message is an exhortation to us to live a certain type of life, and an exhortation to put these things into practice.
>
> But that is an utter travesty of the gospel. The Christian gospel in the first instance does not ask us to do anything. It first of all proclaims and announces to us what God has done for us. The first statement of the gospel is not an exhortation to action or to conduct and behavior. Before man is called upon to do anything, he must have received something. Before God calls upon a man to put anything into practice, He has made it possible for man to put it into practice.[33]

---

[33] David Martyn Lloyd-Jones, *Expository Sermons on Second Peter* (Carlisle, PA: The Banner of Truth Trust, 1983), 23–24.

There is order that is vital: since we each have a wonderful identity by virtue of our union with Christ freely given the moment we are converted, our doings are based on what God has done for us in Christ on the front end. There is no more need to earn what we already have been given by grace in Christ.

Repent and Believe the Gospel

Paul exhorts the Christian to "take every thought captive to obey Christ" (2 Corinthians 10:4–5). Take that annoying, humming lie that is no longer true of you and renounce it as false. Don't obey those impulses within to try to prove you are a condemned sinner or a worthless loser. Repent of those foolish strategies that never worked and were only attempts to save your reputation, except to make you ultimately feel defeated, worn out, and vulnerable to bad habits. Then, preach the gospel to yourself (Psalm 42:5), and trust it is true. Preach to yourself, says Lloyd-Jones, in a way like this:

> You have to take yourself in hand … You must turn on yourself, upbraid yourself, condemn your [mood], exhort yourself and say to yourself, "Hope thou in God"—instead of muttering in this depressed, unhappy way.[34]

With regard to projecting your lie about yourself on to others, as if they thought the same about you, I suggest you asking others questions of clarification to avoid unfair accusations of their thoughts and motives. Perhaps you will discover they never thought such a thing, and they were only projecting their false identities on you!

---

[34] Martin Lloyd-Jones, *Spiritual Depression* (Grand Rapids: Eerdmans, 1990), 21. I have taken the liberty to take out the word *yourself* and replaced it with *your mood*.

Questions for Group Discussion

1. What is your CCT (your central condemning thought) that feels so true about you, but is not from God?
2. When are the times when you are most vulnerable to believe Satan's lie about who you are?
3. What foolish strategies have you come up with to prove you are better than this?
4. How have they worked?
5. Are you sick of them yet?
6. Have you ever surrendered to the lie?
7. Do you believe people cherish their lies?
8. Have you ever projected it on to others, assuming they believe it is who you are?
9. Are you ready to renounce your CCT as a lie?

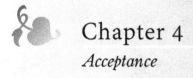

Chapter 4

Acceptance

Christians never stop needing to hear the gospel, and central to the gospel is personally embracing the good news that the announcement we preach to ourselves; namely, "I am justified."

There is nothing more foolish, yet common, than for a Christian to seek to establish a righteousness of his or her own (Romans 10:3). Since Jesus established a perfect righteousness for the Christian, there is no need for this. Christians must ask God to deliver them from an inordinate lust for vindication before the eyes of others. Saint Augustine prayed: "Oh Lord, deliver me from the lust of always having to vindicate myself!"

I have sought to establish my righteousness before others. For example, I attempted to gain house, lawn, and car maintenance righteousness before my father-in-law came to visit us. Anything we work at can become a way we seek to establish our righteousness before God and others—health, environment, etc. It gives a false righteousness, a self-righteousness, to attempt to stand on to make God pleased with us, to divide the world between the good and the bad, and to put ourselves above others.

The Protestant reformation was a revival of the gospel after centuries of the darkness and oppression of religion. Religion, posing as true as true Christianity, functions in three ways: (1) to put our good works before God in order to make Him owe us something; (2) to divide the world in half between the good people and the bad people; and (3) to look down on the bad people as a good person (Luke 18:9–14).

The gospel is our best ammunition against Satan's lies and condemning accusations, but religion still seems to remain many Christians' weapon of choice. This is because our default mode, like a computer printer, will execute religion unless we disobey the impulsive urge of religion and select the gospel mode of operational living. Frankly, I do not see this happening without memorizing a short definition of justification—justification by grace through faith in Christ alone.

If a pastor asked a large congregation of Christians on any given Sunday, "What does justification mean?" very few (if any) hands would be raised to answer the question. Why was Abraham credited righteous when he was a sinner? Why was Joshua the high priest in filthy rags and accused by Satan as such covered with white garments? Why did Jesus come to seek not the righteous but the unrighteous? Why did the apostle Paul take so much time arguing for justification by faith in Romans, Corinthians, and Galatians?

What is this vital doctrine? Martin Luther said it is "the article upon which the church stands or falls" (*articulus stantis et cadentis ecclesiae*).[35] John Calvin asserted that justification is "the principal hinge" upon which Christianity is supported, "For unless you understand first of all what your position is before God, and what the judgment [is] which He passes upon you, you have no foundation on which your salvation can be laid, or on which your godly approach can be reared."[36]

---

[35] Martin Luther, *What Luther Says: An Anthology*, ed. Ewald M. Plass, 3 vols. (St Louis, MO: Concordia Publishing, 1959), Vol. 2, 704 n5.

[36] John Calvin, *Institutes of the Christian Religion*, 2 vols., trans. Henry Beverage (1845; reprint, Grand Rapids, MI: Eerdmans, 1964), Vol. 2, 37 (3.11.1).

The teaching of scripture tells us who we are in Christ. When we trust Christ for our justification, we trust that: (1) we are pardoned of all our sins; (2) we are accepted as righteous in God's sight; (3) but only for the righteousness of Christ imputed to us, and received by faith alone.

When Jesus Christ lived thirty-three years of perfect righteousness, that active righteousness was what was imputed or credited to the Christian. The Christian's imperfect self-righteousness, which is as filthy rags, and unrighteousness were taken upon Jesus on the cross so that He suffered the penalty our self-righteousness and unrighteousness deserves, and we receive and become the righteousness of God in Christ. (I always want to write this in all capitals and add exclamation marks.)

Scriptural support abounds with this gospel truth. Abraham was credited as righteous when he believed God's promise (Genesis 15:6). Paul taught that all have fallen short of God's righteousness, but Christ's righteousness alone is our basis for acceptance with God as righteous (Romans 3:22–28, 4:5, 5:1; Acts 13:38–39; Galatians 2:14–16; Philippians 3:8–9). "For our sake God made him to be sin who knew no sin," Paul explains, "so that in him we might become the righteousness of God" (2 Corinthians 5:21). God declares the ungodly righteous, but only for the righteousness of Christ imputed to them. He became sin that we might become the righteousness of God. There is no more need to establish a righteousness of our own. There is no more condemnation for those who are in Christ Jesus (Romans 8:1). There is no more need for justifying ourselves before God and others.

Memorize This Prayer as Your Daily Bread

> I am pardoned of all my sins and accepted as righteous in His sight, but only for the righteousness

of Christ imputed to me and received by faith alone.[37]

Take a few minutes to memorize this prayer (use hand motions) by praying it out loud to God over and over again. Then you will have the greatest weapon when condemning thoughts come to your mind. Once you memorize this prayer based on the doctrine of justification, you can live the Christian life without the ups and downs internally. You won't obey the internal impulses to prove and defend yourself as righteous when you're not, nor surrender to the lie when you are aware of your unrighteousness. You can live by faith based upon the righteousness of another—namely, Christ's righteousness.

On Our Best Days and on Our Worst Days

Alright, let's suppose you had a terrible day. It was one of your worst, and your core lie (CCT) feels so true that it threatens to rule you. You woke up to hearing that you forgot to buy orange juice and coffee on the way home from work yesterday, and your family expressed what a disappointment you have been lately. You couldn't focus on prayer or Bible reading, and you were late to work. Your boss came to your desk to show you what your mistake cost the company and left without saying anything. In the silence evil beat you down more. You were tempted to project your lie on to everyone at work—that they viewed you as a failure. Your friend at work got a promotion, and your kids misbehaved that night at home. As you put your head on your pillow that night, however, you prayed: "I am pardoned of

[37] This is based on *The Westminster Confession of Faith*, Shorter Catechism Question/Answer #33, (Philadelphia, PA: Great Commission Publications, 1989), 74.

all my sins and accepted as righteous in Your sight, but only for the righteousness of Christ imputed to me and received by faith alone."

Justification keeps you from self-hatred, depression, shame, and guilt. It keeps you moving forward to love others well without pulling them into your lair of lies and victimization. It is your staying power and defense on your worst days, but it is also your spiritual thermostat to keep your arrogance low on your best days.

Okay, let's suppose you had your best day in a long time. After your morning time in the Bible and prayer, you made breakfast for your wife and children. They said, "You are such a godly husband and father!" After arriving to work, your boss called you into his office to tell you that you made the big difference this year, and that you will have a forthcoming pay raise. You lead a coworker to Christ at lunch, coach your child's soccer team in the afternoon, and put your children to bed with a blessing. As you lay your head down on your pillow that night, you pray: "I am pardoned of all my sins and accepted as righteous in Your sight, *but only for the righteousness of Christ* imputed to me and received by faith alone."

This is the article upon which you stand or fall; it is the hinge upon which your position before God and the world hangs no matter what your Christian performance was like that day. Milton Vincent writes:

> The gospel also reminds me that my righteous standing with God always holds firm regardless of my performance, because my standing is based solely on the work of Jesus and not mine. On my worst days of sin and failure the gospel encourages me with God's unrelenting grace toward me. On my best days of victory and usefulness, the gospel

keeps me relating to God solely on the basis of Jesus' righteousness and not mine.[38]

Do you believe that God is pleased with you, with a Christian in union with Christ? Does God favor you or not when you are united to Christ? Do you know that unless you are fortified with the gospel you are in danger of setting up your performance as the key to making God love you? This is what Luther was concerned with. "If we doubt or do not believe that God is gracious and pleased with us, or if we presumptuously expect to please Him through our works," Luther argued, "then all [efforts to comply to the Law] is pure deception, outwardly honoring God, but inwardly setting up self as a false savior."[39] Therefore, it is "necessary is it that we know this article well, teach it to others, and beat it into their heads continually."[40]

The Key to Identity in Christ

What is the most important thing we can do after renouncing the lies and condemning thoughts? It is to turn our eyes up, outside of ourselves, and to see Christ with adoring love and admiration. "The evangelical orientation is inward and subjective," writes Sinclair Ferguson. "We are far better at looking inward than we are at looking outward. Instead, we need to expend our energies

---

[38] Milton Vincent, *A Gospel Primer for Christians: Learning to See the Glories of God's Love* (Nashville, TN: Thomas Nelson, 2008), 20.

[39] Martin Luther, On First Commandment in *Works of Martin Luther with Introductions and Notes* (Pantianos Classics, 1915), Vol. 1, 197.

[40] Martin Luther, *St. Paul's Epistle to the Galatians* (Philadelphia: Smith, English & Co., 1860), 206.

admiring, exploring, expositing, and extolling Jesus Christ."[41] This is the gospel theme in one of our contemporary hymns:

> When Satan tempts me to despair,
> upward I look and see Him there.[42]

Ponder another gospel hymn writer and preacher from the nineteenth century:

> To be entitled to use another's name, when my own name is worthless; to be allowed to wear another's raiment, because my own is torn and filthy; to appear before God in another's person—the person of the Beloved Son—this is the summit of all blessing.[43]

> The sin-bearer and I have exchanged names, robes, and persons! I am now represented by Him, my own personality having disappeared; He now appears in the presence of God for me. All that makes Him precious and dear to the Father has been transferred to me.

> His Excellency and glory are seen as if they were mine; and I receive the love, and the fellowship, and the glory as if I had earned them all. So entirely one am I with the sin-bearer, that God treats me not

---

[41] Quoted in C. J. Mahaney's *Living the Cross-Centered Life* (Colorado Springs, CO: Multnomah Books, 2002), 48.

[42] "Before the Throne of God Above" (Public Domain), Text by Charitie Lees Bancroft; Tune by Vikki Cook.

[43] Horatius Bonar, *The Everlasting Righteousness*, (Edinburgh: The Banner of Truth Trust, 1874/1993), 24.

merely as if I had not done the evil that I have done; but as if I had done all the good which I have not done, but which my substitute has done.

In one sense I am still the poor sinner, once under wrath; in another I am altogether righteous and shall be so forever, because of the Perfect One, in whose perfection I appear before God. Nor is this a false pretense or a hollow fiction, which carries no results or blessings with it. It is an exchange which has been provided by the Judge, and sanctioned by law; an exchange of which any sinner upon earth may avail himself and be blest.[44]

Father,
I repent of my righteousness and my unrighteousness. I am pardoned of all my sins and accepted as righteous in Your sight, but only for the righteousness of Christ imputed to me and received by faith alone.
Amen.

Questions for Group Discussion

1. Recite the justification prayer as a group until you memorize it. Would you recite the prayer of justification this week when you end your day, whether it is a good or bad day?
2. What do you love about having a new identity in Christ?

---

[44] Ibid., 44–45.

Chapter 5
No Longer Fatherless

A Christian owns his status as a child, and confesses: "I was chosen in love by God to be adopted as His child." What a happy confession of a Christian, who is secure in his or her identity in Christ!

"Doctor Bob, could you speak to our children before you preach to the pastors?" This request by the host pastor was asked on our way during a pastor's conference in Kinshasa, Democratic Republic of Congo. When we turned the corner, I was shocked to see some three hundred street children sitting with a tiny cup of tea and little piece of bread in each their hands, which the church had given them. Gazing at them, my heart just broke, and through the tears I spoke on how our Father in heaven loves orphans. He chooses them in love to be His very own children to the praise of His glorious grace.

Dr. Bob Peterson, pastor of Covenant Presbyterian Church in Naples, Florida, has told his story of what it was like to be an orphan until his teen years, and what it felt like to be unwanted.[45] He tells how he rescued his sister from being taken advantage of by another man, who later beat his wife to death with a hammer. Peterson said he was put into a foster home and was still wetting his bed. His foster

---

[45] Robert Peterson, *The Theater of Angels: Redeeming Affliction* (Covenant Books, 2015), 4–6, 216–22.

care mother had enough, so she hung a big square of cardboard sign on a rope around his neck and made him stand on the front porch. The sign read, "This boy still wets the bed."[46] All his classmates saw him as they walked by on their way to school. "After that," Peterson wrote, "I was teased mercifully. Almost everyone called me Bobby Bedwetter."[47]

Bob ended up with his sister under the care of the State Welfare Department. When Mary Peterson was looking for a little boy and girl, the social workers warned Mary, "These kids have been through the system. By this age, most of them are damaged goods." The social workers brought out a photo album of five hundred kids, and Mary had a love at first sight for Bob and his sister, Kim. "That's the little boy and girl that I want," she said as she continued to gaze at her future son and daughter.[48]

The day came to meet the Mary and Arnold Peterson. The social worker gave a harsh warning: "Don't mess this up. As old as you are, you may never get another chance at being adopted." The two siblings got into the car and went to a bowling alley. Bob wrote: "I figured that if I bowled a strike they would want to adopt me for sure. As hard as I tried, almost every ball ended up in the gutter. I was sure that I had blown my chances." After messing up with chopsticks at a Chinese restaurant, Mary began to clap her hands, and Arnold gave Bob a gift. Arnold said, "Bobby, would you like to be my son?"[49]

This was Bob's introduction to grace. Dr. Bob Peterson is a delightful and effective preacher of the gospel now, and I believe he knows firsthand about the doctrine of being chosen in love as a child of God.

Adoption is an act of God's free grace to choose us in love to be

---

[46] Ibid., 6.

[47] Ibid.

[48] Ibid., 217.

[49] Ibid., 218–19.

His sons and daughters; to have His name put on us; to give His Spirit to dwell in us; to care for us as a perfect Father; to grant us every privilege of children; and to make us heirs of all that He promises, and fellow heirs with Christ in glory through our suffering with Him. It is this act of God's grace by which we become His children, and He becomes our Father. In fact, the identity of the Father and the Son is the central desire of the Holy Spirit. This is because, in the words of the cofounder of Together for Adoption, "This identity is central to who they are."[50] God the Father is an adopting Father, the Son is an elder Brother, and the Spirit witnesses with us that we are God's adopted children (Romans 8:15–16).

The scriptures are filled with this concept. In the Old Testament, God refers to Israel as His son whom He called out of Egypt. We are adopted sons and daughters, by which we cry: "Abba! Father!" We experience the witness of the Spirit that we are God's beloved children, who were chosen in love to the praise of His glorious grace. Since Jesus is God's only begotten Son, He delights in bringing many sons to glory through His suffering (Romans 8:14–17, 23; Galatians 4:4; Ephesians 1:3; 1 John 3:1; Hebrews 2:10). Jesus's use of the phrase *your Father* is pervasive in His Sermon on the Mount.

The Father's legal act begins with acceptance and then proceeds with loving support. Not only does He accept us as pardoned and righteous, but He also comes down from the Judge's bench and puts His arm around us and says, as it were, "Now, I have great plans to enlarge My family. I am taking you to My home in glory even now, and I am going to provide for your every need. And I want you to learn to call Me Abba_Father." Whereas justification is forensic, adoption belongs to the domestic world of love. Whereas adoption gives us family status, in regeneration He gives us the nature fitting for being His beloved child (John 1:12, 3:3). We begin to show an

---

[50] Dan Cruver in the Foreword to Joel R. Beeke's *Heirs with Christ: The Puritans on Adoption* (Grand Rapids, MI: Reformation Heritage Books, 2008), xi.

outward evidence of our sonship (Romans 8:14). We are delivered from slavish fear and rise up out of crowd when we recognize God as our Father and cry out (Romans 8:15), "Father!" Our obedience to our Father is no longer motivated by "a slavish fear," but with a childlike love and willing mind according to the Puritan pastor-theologians of the Westminster Assembly in the 1640s.

Sometimes the children who do not have our nature or our adoption status will show cruelty on the playgrounds of life. One adopted school boy was tormented for being adopted by his classmates day after day, but one day the child turned to his tormenters and asked: "Do you know what the real difference is between you all and myself?" For once the other children were dumbfounded. He answered his own question, saying: "Well, the really big difference is this. My parents went through a lot of trouble to choose me, but your parents had to get along with whoever they got!" This is true of us as well, and when we get to heaven, there will not be one of us there who is not adopted, except our elder Brother Jesus. Jesus shall not at all be ashamed to call us brothers and sisters forever (Hebrews 2:11).

Why Is This So Practical When It Comes to Obedience?

If you want to learn how much people embrace the gospel, be curious about what they think of being God's children and having God as their Father. If this is not the identity that fuels their worship and prayer and his perspective on life, it may be a clear indication that they know little of the love of God within.

We have a new motivation for obeying our Father in heaven, for to be motivated by the threats of the law is pre or sub Christian. In fact, as Charles Spurgeon found, the more we view God as a kind Father, the less motivated we'll be to disobey His commands:

> While I regarded God as a tyrant I thought my sin a trifle; but when I knew Him to be my Father, then I mourned that I could ever have kicked against Him. When I thought God was hard, I found it easy to sin; but when I found God so kind, so good, so overflowing with compassion, I smote upon my breast to think that I could ever have rebelled against One who loved me so, and sought my good.[51]

We have assurance and confidence that we are adorable to Him, even in our imperfect efforts to live in His family and serve His good purposes. "Such children ought we to be," wrote John Calvin, "firmly trusting that our services will be approved by our most merciful Father, however small, rude, and imperfect these may be."[52] As the old hymn writer, Augustus Toplady put it:

> The terrors of the law and God with me can have nothing to do; My Savior's obedience and blood hide all my transgressions from view.[53]

Are you acting like a child or an orphan?

One consistent lie of the enemy whispers that we are not loved and that we are unwanted, like an orphan all alone in the world. If you act out of that lie, you'll be miserable in trying to earn God's love already there. When do you act like an orphan, and when have you felt most like an orphan?

Wilbur Chapman, the famous evangelist, told of a father who

---

[51] Charles H. Spurgeon, *Repentance After Conversion*, Sermon No. 2419, June 12, 1887.

[52] John Calvin, *Institutes*, 3.19.5, Vol. 1, 837.

[53] Augustus Toplady, "A Debtor to Mercy Alone" in *Gospel Magazine*, 1771 (Public Domain).

searched for years for his lost son. The son acted like an unwanted orphan, hitting every businessman with a nice suit up for a dime. He would tug on their coat sleeve and say, "Excuse me, sir, but may I have a dime?" One day his wealthy father, after years of searching for his son, stood on a train station platform in a major city. He felt a tug on his coat and heard a young man say, "Excuse me, sir, may I have a dime?" The father turned, and there he was, face-to-face with his son. He said to his beloved son: "A dime? I have been searching for you all these years to give you everything I have!"

It is an amazing truth that Jesus came to bring us to the Father, and He taught us to pray to the Father because all the resources and power and love of the Father are channeled to His dear sons and daughters through His Son's merits.

Questions for Group Discussion

1. Have you been living like an orphan at times?
2. How does your Father in heaven view your baby steps of obedience as you learn to walk before Him?
3. How does seeing God the Father's smiling face looking at you motivate your obedience to Him?

Chapter 6

Set Apart as Special to God

When a person becomes a Christian, he or she is immediately and once for all sanctified, although the process of becoming holy follows in his or her experience. A Christian admits, "I am a saint—holy and empowered by the Holy Spirit."

One of Satan's biggest lies in Western (American) contemporary culture is embraced when, as Christians, we surrender and say, "I am a victim." Criminals in America often believe that any court in the land would excuse them, if only they understood that they were a victim of an early crime, drug effects, etc. Christians today can easily be conformed into the culture's mold by embracing this lie and justifying self-centeredness. It is an easy step, out of this false identity, to give into lust, sinful anger, and transgressions and to justify this behavior with excuses and blame shifting. When we readily excuse our failure to love well or pursue holiness, it is obvious that we are not embracing our true identities in Christ. In order to be more than conquerors, we need large doses of the gospel.

There is nothing more than the gospel, but there is a lot more of it! What a thrill to find out who we are in Christ, and to renounce the lies that may once have been true of us in the past! In this chapter we learn that our identities in Christ are beyond positional truths, like justification. As saints, something existential took place when we were united to Christ by faith. There was a radical, definitive breach with our old self (man). We were not only counted righteous (justified), but the gospel tells me more good news; namely, we were *constituted* holy.

When we were united to Christ by faith, the Holy Spirit definitively sanctified us. This one-time work has with it ongoing results. The radical, once-for-all, and irreversible breach with one's sinful nature (old self and identity) is experienced like this: we are holy, we are becoming progressively holy, and one fine day we shall be completely holy (definitively, progressively, and finally consummated).

The Christian is a saint, a holy one. You, as a Christian, can say: "My sin's penalty was removed, sin's power is weakening, and one happy day in heaven sin's presence shall be no more." This important when temptation occurs and one's former sinful ways seem reasonable and strong. It is vital that the Christian not see himself or herself as a victim of or slave to one's old self. Experiential power is exercised over sin with biblical weaponry and authority when we embrace our true identities in Christ (2 Corinthians 10:4–5).

Sanctification is generally thought of as a process, and there is certainly a sense in which it is. The New Testament, however, also frequently represents the Christian as one who has been sanctified and therefore as one who has been definitively constituted in some way and on some basis as holy (see Acts 20:32; 26:18; 1 Corinthians 1:2; 6:11; Ephesians 5:26). The term used to describe our identities is sanctified. It is used in the perfect tense of αγιαζω, hagiazō in the first three references above, and the aorist tense in the last two references. There are, in addition to these, numerous instances where Christians are called "saints" or "holy ones."

What does this mean that, as Christians, we have new identities as saints? It means that the old self is dead, and a new self is alive.

As Romans 6:2, 6 puts it: "We died [ἀπεθάνομεν, apethanomen] to sin … the old man was crucified [συνεσταυρώθη, synestaurōthē] [with him]." It means: "You have been set free [ἐλευθερωθέντες, eleutherōthentes] from sin and have become slaves [ἐδουλώθητε, edoulōthete] to righteousness" (Romans 6:18). It means that "now we have been released [κατηργήθημεν, katērgēthēmen] from the law, having died [ἀποθανόντες, apothanontes] to that by which we were bound" (Romans 7:4–6)." It means: "That we, having died [ἀπογενόμενοι, apogenomenoi] to sins, might live to righteousness" (1 Peter 2:24).[54]

Through its language of death and of liberation from slavery, this biblical material depicts a radical contrast between the believer's pre-Christian existence and the life he lives as a Christian. It affirms that every Christian is definitively sanctified the moment he trusts in Christ (see Acts 26:18: "those having been sanctified by faith which is in me"). He died to sin, and he has been liberated from sin. Accordingly, the scriptures speak of every Christian as a "saint" or "holy one" (ὁ ἅγιος, ho hagios; see, e.g., Ephesians 1:1; Philippians 1:1; Colossians 1:2).

This sustained contrast can only mean that for the Christian there exists:

> A cleavage, a breach, a translation as really and decisively true in the sphere of [spiritual] relationship as in the ordinary experience of death. There is a once-for-all definitive and irreversible breach with the realm in which sin reigns in and

---

[54] 1 Peter 4:1–2: "Therefore, since Christ suffered [παθόντος, pathontos] in the flesh, arm yourselves also with the same mind, because he who has suffered [ὁ παθών, ho pathōn] in the flesh [a reference to the Christian who 'suffered in the flesh' when Christ 'suffered in the flesh'] is done with sin, with the result that no longer does he live the rest of his time in the flesh to the lusts of men but to the will of God."

unto death ... In respect of every criterion by which moral and spiritual life is to be assessed, there is absolute differentiation. This means that there is a decisive and definitive breach with the power and service of sin in the case of everyone who has come under the control of the provisions of grace.[55]

Whereas the ground of the Christian's justification is Christ's imputed obedience, the ground of the Christian's definitive sanctification is his real spiritual union with Christ in his death, burial, and resurrection (Romans 6:1–14; 2 Corinthians 5:14–15), into which every Christian is actually brought the moment he becomes a partaker of Christ through faith. In other words, not only is the Christian counted by God as righteous, he is also constituted holy by God's Spirit. It is not simply positional holiness that is envisioned by definitive sanctification: it is a real existential breach with the reign and mastery of sin, which is as decisive and definite as are Christ's death and resurrection.[56] John Murray emphasizes the ongoing consequences our new identities bring us:

It is just because we cannot allow for any reversal or repetition of Christ's death on the tree that we cannot allow for any compromise on the doctrine that every believer has died to sin and no longer lives under its dominion. Sin no longer lords it over him ... Likewise the decisive and definitive entrance upon newness of life in the case of every believer is required by the fact that the resurrection of Christ was decisive and definitive. As we cannot allow for

[55] John Murray, "Definitive Sanctification," in *Collected Writings of John Murray* (Edinburgh, 1977), Vol. 2, 79–80.

[56] See Robert Reymond, *A New Systematic Theology of the Christian Faith* (Nashville, TN: Nelson, 1998), 756–59.

any reversal or repetition of the resurrection, so we cannot allow for any compromise on the doctrine that every believer is a new man, that the old man has been crucified, that the body of sin has been destroyed, and that, as a new man in Christ Jesus, he serves God in the newness which is none other than that of the Holy Spirit of whom he has become the habitation and his body the temple.[57]

Although, as a Christian, you are holy and anointed a saint, it does not mean that you actually achieve, personally and existentially, sinless perfection the moment you trusted Christ; this would leave no room for progressive sanctification. Besides, complete and final sanctification awaits the coming of our Lord Jesus Christ (1 Thessalonians 5:23). The Christian who says he has no sin is deceiving himself and the truth is not in him (1 John 1:8). What it does mean is that every Christian, the moment he or she becomes a Christian by virtue of his or her union with Christ, is instantly constituted a "saint" and enters into a new relationship with respect to the former reign of sin in his life and with God himself. Your identity is no longer that of a slave to sin, but a holy servant of Christ.[58]

Questions for Group Discussion

1. How does a victim mentality make us justify our sinful behaviors?
2. How does it help us to embrace our identities as saints before we start our day?
3. What has the Holy Spirit given you that made your identity in Christ an empowered life?

---

[57] John Murray, "Definitive Sanctification," 289, 293.

[58] The apostle Paul's own assurance is that "sin will not lord it over him" (Romans 6:14).

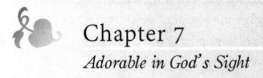

Chapter 7
Adorable in God's Sight

We all long for glory and fall short of the glory of God. The way to glorification for us is a work of God and will take place on the last day for Christians. When we dwell on His glory, we behold Christ. His glory is the brightness and the nature of the Creator of the universe. "He is the radiance of the glory of God and the exact imprint of his nature, and he upholds the universe by the word of his power" (Hebrews 1:3).

His glory is the sum of all the beauties of love and wisdom and power that he revealed in his earthly life. "And the Word became flesh and dwelt among us, and we have seen his glory" (John 1:14a). His glory is the triumph of every battle he wins over all his personal, global, and universal enemies. We will worship Christ with loud voices, saying: "Worthy is the Lamb who was slain, to receive power and wealth and wisdom and might and honor and glory and blessing" (Revelation 5:12)! His glory is the eternal radiance of the light of God replacing the sun and moon forever. "And the city has no need of sun or moon to shine on it, for the glory of God gives it light, and its lamp is the Lamb" (Revelation 21:23).

We were made for this glory. This alone will satisfy the longings of your heart. Jesus prayed that we would see His glory in its fullness, on the other side of His resurrection: "Father, I desire that they also, whom you have given me, may be with me where I am, to see my glory" (John 17:24).

Now in 2 Thessalonians 2:14 Paul says we are destined for "the possession of the glory of our Lord Jesus Christ." The glory of Christ is our "blessed hope." We long for him to appear. "We wait for our blessed hope, the appearing of the glory of our great God and Savior Jesus Christ" (Titus 2:13).

When it appears—when He appears shining with it—we will see Him more truly, more clearly, more compellingly, more emotionally, more attentively, and more undividedly than we have ever seen anything or anyone—good or evil. All the good emotions we have ever known, and all the good aspects of all the unpleasant emotions, will come together in the fearful, unprecedented joy of that sight.

Then we will be changed in a moment, in the twinkling of an eye, and we will become glorious, as He is glorious. The sight of His incomparable glory will change us into His glorious likeness. "When he appears we shall be like him, because we shall see him as he is" (1 John 3:2). For now, we suffer with him. But this happens "in order that we may also be glorified with him" (Romans 8:17).

Our union with Him will be changed from invisible to visible. And in Him we will become glorious. "God has called you to his eternal glory in Christ" (1 Peter 5:10). The union will be mutually radiant, so that not only are we glorified in Him but also He in us. "The name of our Lord Jesus will be glorified in you, and you in him" (2 Thessalonians 1:12). Jesus Himself will always be the height and the depth of our glory and our joy.

Thus, we will be "conformed to the image of his Son" (Romans 8:29), which means that we will not only be given the radiance of the Son, but the character of the Son—the heart-eyes of the Son. With this character and these heart-eyes, we will be able to see and enjoy the gift of the Son's radiance in us, and the gift of the Son's radiance before us, in such a way that our own radiance will never tempt us to think we are God. He Himself will always be the height and the depth of our glory and our joy.

Possessing Glory through Our Lord Jesus Christ

Union with Christ—if His resurrection is the first fruits of what we are a part of, then it absolutely guarantees my perseverance. In 2 Corinthians 4:17 it says: "Our light affliction, which is but for a moment, is working for us a far more exceeding and eternal weight of glory." No vessel can be made of gold without fire, so it is unlikely that we can be made glorious unless we are melted and refined in the furnace of affliction and of trial.[59]

The Christian doctrine of glorification is stunning, to say the least. Not only will we see Jesus in all His new-creation glory, but we will share with Him in it. "When he appears we shall be like him, because we shall see him as he is" (1 John 3:2).

If the scriptures didn't make it so plain, an honest author wouldn't have the boldness to make this up, even in one's wildest imagination. The apostle Paul, however, tells us we "will appear with him in glory" (Colossians 3:3), and that awaiting us is "an eternal weight of glory" (2 Corinthians 4:16). Jesus Himself prays to the Father about our being adorable to God (John 17:22), and perhaps most shocking of all, Peter says we will "became partakers of the divine nature" (2 Peter 1:4).

We initially may object and reason that this is only about God's glory, not ours. Ponder this, however, that the more we are transformed into the likeness of His glory the more Christ is glorified in us. The second coming will be the public vindication of the justification, adoption, sanctification, and glorification we have already received.

In light of humanity's eternal destiny in heaven or in hell, C. S.

---

[59] See Thomas Watson, *Puritan Gems; or, the Wise and Holy Sayings of Thomas Watson* (GLH Publishing. Kindle Edition), (2012-11-20), 22.

Lewis reminds us to treat others not based upon one's appearance now but then. In his awesome sermon entitled "The Weight of Glory," Lewis stated:

> It is a serious thing to remember that the dullest and most uninteresting person you talk to may one day be a creature which, if you saw it now, you would be strongly tempted to worship, or else a horror and a corruption such as you now meet, if at all, only in a nightmare. All day long we are, in some degree helping each other to one or the other of these destinations. It is in the light of these overwhelming possibilities, it is with the awe and the circumspection proper to them, that we should conduct all our dealings with one another, all friendships, all loves, all play, all politics. There are no ordinary people. You have never talked to a mere mortal ... But it is immortals whom we joke with, work with, marry, snub, and exploit—immortal horrors or everlasting splendors."[60]

Questions for Group Discussion

1. How does God view you, since you are glorified in Christ?
2. How did C. S. Lewis's words affect your thinking in his sermon "The Weight of Glory"?
3. Do you believe that one day God will adore you made into the likeness of Christ as you are beholding His glory at the same time?
4. Why is this good news hard for us to embrace?

---

[60] C. S. Lewis, *The Weight of Glory* (New York: HarperOne, 2001), 45–46.

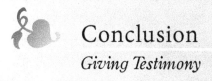

Conclusion
Giving Testimony

Now it is time to share your identity with others. If you are participating in a group with this book, then this is the time for each person to go around the room and share his or her identity in Christ with one another. First, see my sample of how I wrote out my identity in Christ, and then take time to write it out using the template below.

Sample

Name and Genealogy

I am Robert Davis Smart. Robert means "man of renown," Davis is after Uncle Len, and the Smarts were from Glasgow and Edinburgh, Scotland. I have a ceaseless generational flow of preachers from my great-grandfather back to the 1600s in Scotland to the 1900s in Vermont, where my grandfather was a preacher's kid. I am a descendant of three members of the Mayflower, yet my recent genealogy includes an uncle and aunt addicted to alcohol. I grew up the youngest of six along Lake Michigan and came to faith in Christ my last year at Purdue University.

Image, Gender, and Brokenness

I am a glorious ruin. I bear God's glory as a man designed to penetrate His creation and lead His people as a pastor, my family as a husband, father, and grandfather, and all peoples as a preacher, writer, and missionary with tender strength in order to give the gospel, cultivate a culture of grace, and leave a legacy for His glory. I am a broken man, who is marred by a constant sense of inadequacy, an arrogant commitment to autonomy, and a deceitful heart that believes Satan's lie that I am unwanted.

Renouncing Lie and Foolish Strategies

I renounce the lie that I am unwanted and mistreated, along with my foolish strategies of self-hatred and pleas for rescue. I preach the gospel to myself each day that I am wanted as significant in my community.

Justified

I am pardoned for all my sins, accepted as righteous in His sight (but only for the righteousness of Christ, received by faith alone). I am justified and vindicated by my Advocate before the Father and Satan as innocent, debt-free, and accepted.

Adopted

I am wanted by my Father and was chosen to be His son in Christ before time and creation to enjoy all the privileges of sonship—prayer, inheritance, provision, protection, support, involvement, His

Name, Christ as my Brother, etc. His Spirit within me tells me this is true and assures me of His love.

Definitively Sanctified

I am a saint, a holy person, who is set apart for God's special purposes. I am baptized with the Holy Spirit, gifted, indwelt by, and sealed with the Holy Spirit, who has made a once-for-all radical breach with my sinful nature. He intercedes with groans within me so that all things work together for my good.

Sharing My Identity in Christ

My name is _____ (full name). I am the son/ daughter of _____, the grandson/granddaughter of _____ and _____ (give brief explanation). I am the husband/wife of _____ and the father/mother of _____.

I am made in the image of God, which means I am _____. I am a fallen image bearer too, and therefore a "glorious ruin."

I am a man/woman, and not a woman/man, which means my glory as a man/woman is expressed by _____. I am a broken man/woman, which means the curse in Genesis 3 was meant to make me long for another Man (Jesus) to save and change me into His likeness.

My brokenness is seen in the way I _____.

I renounce my core lie and Satan's condemning thought that I am _____, and I renounce my foolish and autonomous strategies to overcome this lie—also my surrender to this lie from time to time. These foolish strategies, which did and do not work, are _____.

I am pardoned of all my sins and declared righteous in God's sight, but only for the righteousness of Christ imputed to me and received by faith alone, which means I am justified.

I am the son/daughter of God the Father, who chose me in love to be adopted into His family through Jesus. And I cry out for intimacy with Him through the Holy Spirit; saying, "Abba! Father!"

I am a saint, a holy one, a consecrated man/woman for holiness of life and calling. I am anointed with the Holy Spirit and gifted with spiritual gifts of love, power, and effective service in all of life and every relationship. I am a new creature in Christ and declare war with my old, sinful nature in the irreconcilable war that lasts until heaven (definitively sanctified).

For ongoing interaction and more resources, please see my blog at http://www.identityinChrist.co.

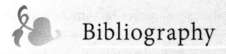

Bibliography

Allender, Dan B. *To Be Told*. Colorado Springs, CO: Waterbrook Press, 2005.

Bancroft, Charitie Lees. "Before the Throne of God Above" (Public Domain), Text by Charitie Lees Bancroft; Tune by Vikki Cook.

Bavinck, Herman. *Reformed Dogmatics*. Grand Rapids, MI: Baker Academic, 2004, volume 2.

Bonar, Horatius, *The Everlasting Righteousness*. Edinburgh: The Banner of Truth Trust, 1874/1993.

Calvin, John. *Institutes of The Christian Religion*. Philadelphia, PA: The Westminster Press, 1960, two volumes.

_____, *Institutes of the Christian Religion*, 2 vols., trans. Henry Beverage. 1845; reprint, Grand Rapids, MI: Eerdmans, 1964, volume 2.

Crabb, Larry. *Men & Women: Enjoying the Difference*. Grand Rapids, MI: Zondervan, 1991.

Crespon, Orlando. *Being Latino in Christ: Finding Wholeness in Your Ethnic Identity.* Downers Grove, IL: InterVarsity Press, 2003.

Cowper, William. *God Moves in Mysterious Ways His Wonders to Perform,* explained at Gospel Coalition website: https://www.thegospelcoalition.org/article/god-moves-in-a-mysterious-way.

Cruver, Dan. "Foreword," in Joel R. Beeke's *Heirs with Christ: The Puritans on Adoption.* Grand Rapids, MI: Reformation Heritage Books, 2008.

DeFranza, Megan K. *Sex Difference in Christian Theology: male, female, and intersex in the image of God.* Grand Rapids, MI: Eerdmans, 2015.

Driscoll, Mark. *Who Do You Think You Are?: Finding Your True Identity in Christ.* Nashville, TN: Thomas Nelson, 2013.

Eliade, Mircea. *A History of Religious Ideas.* Chicago, IL: The University of Chicago Press, 1982, three volumes.

Keller, Timothy. *The Reason for God.* New York: Dutton, 2008.

Lane, Timothy S. and Paul David Tripp. *Relationships: A Mess Worth Making.* Greensboro, NC: New Growth Press, 2006.

Lewis, C. S. *The Weight of Glory: And Other Addresses.* New York: HarperOne, 2001.

_____, *Prince Caspian.* New York: HarperTrophy, 1951.

Lloyd-Jones, David Martyn. *Expository Sermons on Second Peter.* Carlisle, PA: The Banner of Truth Trust, 1983.

_____, *Spiritual Depression.* Grand Rapids, MI: Eerdmans, 1990.

Luther, Martin. *What Luther Says: An Anthology*, ed. Ewald M. Plass. St Louis, MO: Concordia Publishing, 1959, volume two.

_____, On First Commandment in *Works of Martin Luther with Introductions and Notes.* Pantianos Classics, 1915, volume one.

_____, *St. Paul's Epistle to the Galatians.* Philadelphia, PA: Smith, English & Co., 1860.

Mahaney, C. J. *Living the Cross-Centered Life.* Colorado Springs, CO: Multnomah Books, 2002.

McCord's, Beth, her helpful blog: yourenneagramcoach.com

Murray, John, "Definitive Sanctification," in *Collected Writings of John Murray* (Edinburgh, 1977), volume two.

Myers, Ken, his resources: http://reformedforum. org/20-years-of-the-mars-hill-audio-journal/

Peterson, Robert, *The Theater of Angels: Redeeming Affliction.* Covenant Books, 2015.

Reymond, Robert. *A New Systematic Theology of the Christian Faith.* Nashville, TN: Thomas Nelson, 1998.

Schaeffer, Francis A. *The Complete Works of Francis A. Schaeffer: A Christian Worldview.* Wheaton, IL: Crossway Books, 1982, volume one.

Spurgeon, Charles H. *Repentance After Conversion*. Sermon No. 2419, June 12, 1887.

Smart, Robert Davis. *Embracing Your Identity in Christ: Renouncing Lies and Foolish Strategies*. Bloomington, IN: WestBow Press, 2017.

_____. *Calling to Christ: Where's My Place?* Bloomington, IN: WestBow Press, 2017.

_____. *Intentionality for Christ: What's My Aim?* Bloomington, IN: WestBow Press, 2017.

_____. *Legacy from Christ: What's My Message?* Bloomington, IN: WestBow Press, 2017.

Taylor, Charles. *A Secular Age*. Cambridge, MA: Belknap Press, 2007.

_____. *Philosophical Arguments*. Cambridge, MA: Harvard University Press, 1993.

Toplady, Augustus. "A Debtor to Mercy Alone" in *Gospel Magazine*, 1771 (Public Domain).

Tsui, Bonnie. "Choose Your Own Identity." *The New York Times Magazine* (December 14, 2015), http://www.nytimes.com/2015/12/14/magazine/choose-your-own-identity

Vincent, Milton. *A Gospel Primer for Christians: Learning to See the Glories of God's Love*. Nashville, TN: Thomas Nelson, 2008.

Watson, Thomas. *Puritan Gems; or, the Wise and Holy Sayings of Thomas Watson*. GLH Publishing. Kindle Edition (Public Domain).

The Westminster Confession of Faith, Shorter Catechism Question/ Answer #33. Philadelphia, PA: Great Commission Publications, 1989.

Yarhouse, Mark A. *Understanding Sexual Identity: A Resource for Youth Ministry*. Grand Rapids, MI: Zondervan, 2013.

Appendix 1

Cherishing Lies about Our Identities as Ministry Leaders

Your identity in Christ is foundational for your calling to Christ. Someone might even challenge your sense of identity as a ministry leader and ask, "Who do you think you are?" The number-one cause of all the ills that ministry leaders face may be traced to the leader embracing a lie in the core of his being that is directly opposed to the truth God speaks of his identity; namely, the gospel.

This is why the Father reminded Jesus of His true identity before the ministry's start and why evil's first attack was against Jesus's sense of identity. Before Jesus began His ministry, the Father clearly reminded His Son of His true identity: "You are My beloved Son, in whom I am well pleased."

Immediately afterward Satan attacked Jesus's true identity as the best strategic way to destroy His ministry. "*If* you are the Son of God," Satan said two times in the temptation of Christ. Every ministry leader is bombarded with lies about his or her identity. "I am unwanted," one believes. Another believes, "I am worthless." Of course, evil strikes when the leader is at her most vulnerable moment. After Satan attacked Jesus in the wilderness when He was tired and hungry, it says, "Satan left for a more *opportune* time." The "opportune time" is when the leader is most vulnerable.

Christian leaders are vulnerable to evil. Lies annoy a ministry leader. Lies tempt him to believe that others think ill of him and to believe contemptuous thoughts about himself. A leader may discover he was most effective at the times when he felt the worst about his identity. All the leader's efforts to improve his ministry performance often make matters worse because the attack is against the gospel-given identity of the leader, not his performance per se.

I wish the solutions were as simple as simply telling leaders to stop believing lies about themselves and to start believing the truth about who they are in Christ. Simply repeat a hundred times, "I am not a failure. I am more than a conqueror." Say, "I am not unwanted. I am chosen to be adopted." The problem is that we are not morally neutral in choosing truth over lies. We are already overly bent toward deceit, even deeply committed to deceit. The reason we rarely make it on sheer intellectual and ideological choices and changes is that we cherish lies and the false identities that have been functioning for us as ministry leaders for years in a way that we even attempt to serve God autonomously. We struggle to believe the kindest and sweetest words of affirmation and love from God about our identities in Christ before we attempt to persuade others that it is true for them. Timothy S. Lane and Paul David Tripp warn ministry leaders:

> If I am seeking to get identity from you, I will watch you too closely, listen to you too intently, and need you too fundamentally. I will ride the roller coaster of your best and worst moments and everything in between. And because I am watching you too closely, I will become acutely aware of your weaknesses and failures. I will become overly critical, frustrated, disappointed, hopeless, and angry. I will be angry not because you are a sinner but because you have failed to deliver the one thing

I seek from you: identity. But none of us will ever get the well-being that comes from knowing who we are from our relation-ships. Instead we will be left with damaged relationships filled with hurt, frustration and anger.[61]

Ask God's Spirit of truth to tell you the lie or central condemning thought (CCT) that you have come to believe about yourself. What is the constant, annoying, and condemning message about you that keeps you from enjoying your calling? Ask God how it has functioned for you over the years. How has it impacted others, like your family and friends?

When Leaders Lose Effectiveness and Faith in the Gospel

How sad to lose ourselves in an attempt to prove we are someone we are not through gospel ministry service! Absurdity riddles spiritual leaders because evil's interpretations of us go undetected.

In our most vulnerable moments in life, evil whispers the reason why one experiences tragedy and lack of fulfillment in serving God: "It was your fault! You are such a disappointment." While we make autonomous commitments to avoid such pain again, we easily redouble our efforts to eliminate the condemning false identity that interpreted us in that moment. If we embrace the lie and the autonomous way to prove one is not a disappointment, then our Christian service and spiritual disciplines often become the means to get what we already have in the gospel.

Such an effort, however, may lead to burnout and the loss of the leader's effectiveness in service. Efforts, which are *not* motivated by *God's* gracious interpretation of us, deny of the truth and misuse

---

[61] Timothy S. Lane and Paul David Tripp, *Relationships: A Mess Worth Making* (Greensboro, NC: New Growth Press, 2006), 60.

spiritual disciplines. For God declares His ministry leader a delight but only for the meritorious efforts of Christ Jesus. Since Christ won the Father's pleasure in us as a gift, which we receive by faith, all works to overcome evil's lies, wounds, or accusations in any other way are exercises in absurdity.

People in our lives suffer when a leader embraces a false identity associated with a wound. If he embraces the lie that he is a disappointment, then he is more likely to project unfairly onto others that they believe he is a disappointment. Soon his words are spoken out of wrongly interpreted wounds, causing pain to spread throughout his community.

I've counseled ministry leaders who have tried for years to overcome Satan's lies by their own efforts. Sometimes the pressure on their performance drove them to excessive righteousness (Ecclesiastes 7:16), and other times they simply surrendered to the lie. When we surrender to a false identity, we agree with evil that a lie is true and the gospel is not.

Despair Is the Loss of Confidence that the Gospel Is True

Absurdity! Meaninglessness! Until we get sick and tired of the lie and our futile efforts to overcome evil's counterfeit identity of us, we'll not welcome what the highest court in heaven declares of us— namely, that we are not only pardoned and righteous in God's sight but also chosen as His beloved children.

Solitude is the way to receive good news again, not in more service for God. It is the place of greatest struggle where our souls may come out from hiding and encounter God's voice once more. There, in His presence, one may hear, "You are My son, whom I adore with delight for Christ's sake." Do you believe the truth about you? Ponder this portion of a sermon given by Dr. Martyn Lloyd-Jones:

Here is something, which is truly important, and something which is basic and fundamental to the whole Christian position. The order in which these things are put is absolutely vital. The Apostle does not ask us to do anything until he has first of all emphasized and repeated what God has done for us in Christ. How often have men given the impression that to be Christian means that you display in your life a kind of general belief of faith, and then you add to it virtue and knowledge and charity! To them the Christian message is an exhortation to us to live a certain type of life, and an exhortation to put these things into practice. But that is an utter travesty of the Gospel. The Christian Gospel in the first instance *does not ask us to do anything.* It first of all proclaims and announces to us what *God has done for us.* The first statement of the Gospel is not an exhortation to action or to conduct and behavior. Before man is called upon *to do* anything, he must have *received* something. Before God calls upon a man to put anything into practice, He has made it possible for man to put it into practice."[62]

---

[62] D. Martyn Lloyd-Jones, *Expository Sermons on Second Peter* (Carlisle, PA: Banner of Truth, 1983), 23–24.

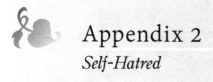

Appendix 2
Self-Hatred

In my life-on-life missional discipleship (LOLMD) group each year, men ask me why it is so hard to receive forgiveness. One reason is that we misunderstand true humility. We assume it is a matter of confessing what wretches we are before God. Often such times of prayer are simply a prayer about how we feel about our failures, but the eyes of our faith are still on our performance of the Christian life.

Confession of sin is one thing, but receiving forgiveness by looking up to Christ's finished work on the cross is another. Jesus looks upon us when we simply hate our sins and ourselves and lifts up focus on Himself and says, "I paid for that. It is finished. You are pardoned."

Self-hatred functions for us in this way: we think that by punishing ourselves, we can improve our performance in the Christian life. Some use it as a way of self-protection. One man thought to himself, *If I beat myself up severely with harsh criticisms, then I'll be able to handle the severe criticisms of others.*

Jesus's love for us on the cross must be received in a way that His acceptance of us is the fuel to enjoy pardon and to love others well through forgiveness, even opening ourselves to pain as we approach them for their welfare and healing.

Appendix 3
Justification[63]

1. Those whom God effectually calls, He also freely justifies—not by infusing righteousness into them, but by pardoning their sins and by accounting and accepting their persons as righteous; not for anything wrought in them, or done by them, but for Christ's sake alone; nor by imputing faith itself, the act of believing, or any other evangelical obedience to them, as their righteousness; but by imputing the obedience and satisfaction of Christ unto them, they receiving and resting on Him and His righteousness by faith; which faith they have not of themselves, it is the gift of God.

2. Faith, thus receiving and resting on Christ and His righteousness, is the alone instrument of justification: yet is it not alone in the person justified, but is ever accompanied with all other saving graces, and is no dead faith, but works by love.

3. Christ, by His obedience and death, did fully discharge the debt of all those who are thus justified, and did make a proper, real, and full satisfaction to His Father's justice in their behalf. Yet,

---

[63] This is adapted from *The Westminster Confession of Faith*, Chapter XI "Of Justification" (Philadelphia, PA: Great Commission Publications, 1989).

in as much as He was given by the Father for them; and His obedience and satisfaction accepted in their stead; and both, freely, not for anything in them; their justification is only of free grace; that both the exact justice, and rich grace of God might be glorified in the justification of sinners.

4. God did, from all eternity, decree to justify all the elect, and Christ did, in the fullness of time, die for their sins, and rise for their justification: nevertheless, they are not justified, until the Holy Spirit doth, in due time, actually apply Christ unto them.

5. God doth continue to forgive the sins of those who are justified; and although they can never fall from the state of justification, yet they may, by their sins, fall under God's fatherly displeasure, and not have the light of His countenance restored unto them, until they humble themselves, confess their sins, beg pardon, and renew their faith and repentance.

6. The justification of believers under the Old Testament was, in all these respects, one and the same with the justification of believers under the New Testament.